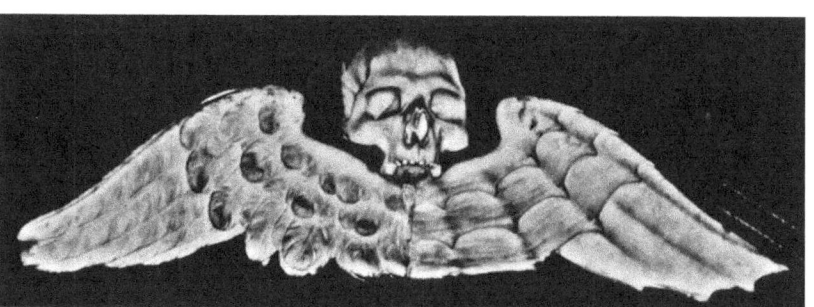

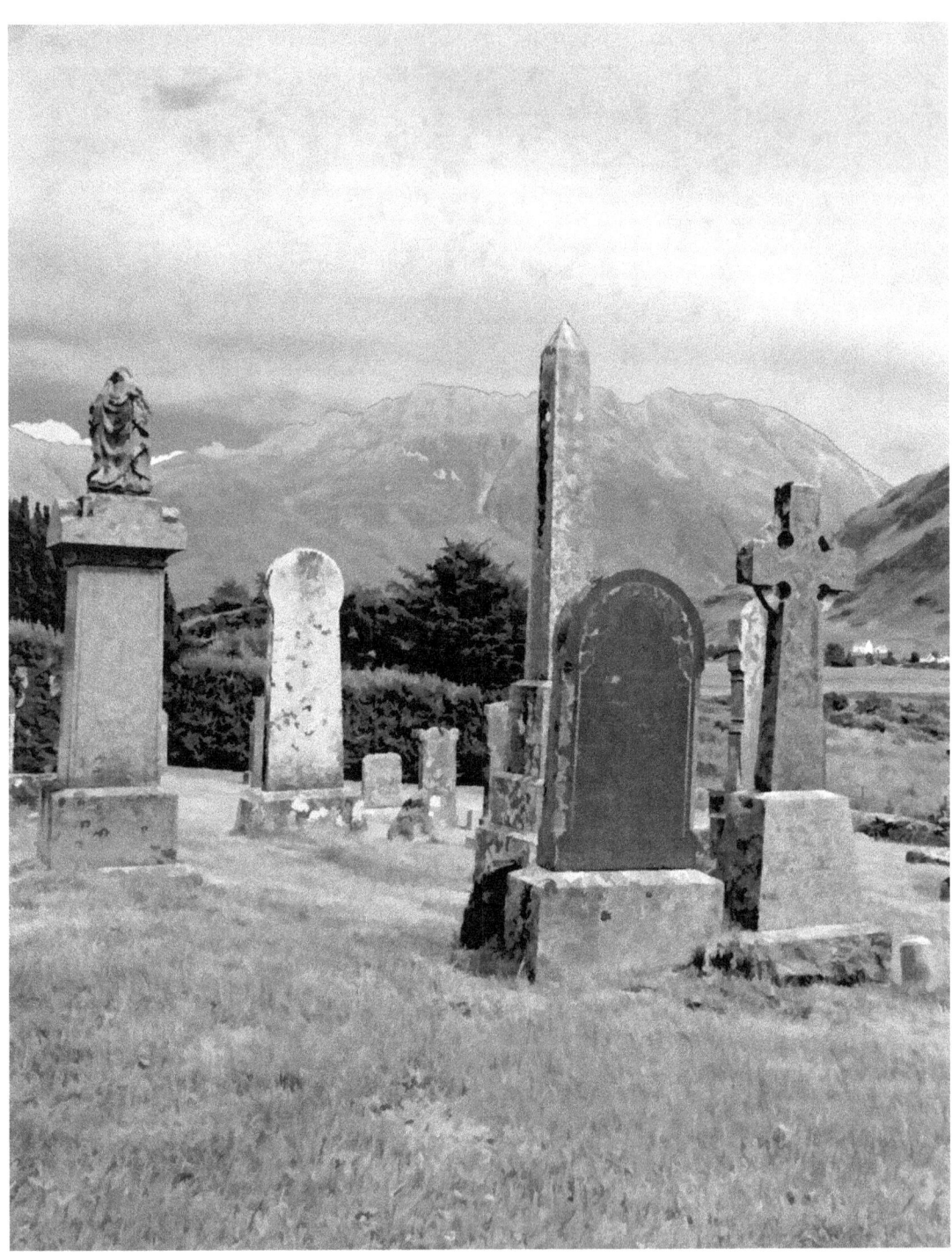

The Art of Death:
Honoring the Craftsmen

Text and Photographs: Traci Law

Law, Traci
The art of death: honoring the craftsmen/by Traci Law

ISBN-13: 978-1492798033
ISBN-10: 1492798037

The idea of burying loved ones after they pass into death is not a new one. Many were buried in simple graves on the family farm, mass graves or in grand structures that have stood the test of time.

Numerous books have been written about the history of cemeteries, burials and the rituals of death but few have displayed the beauty of the artwork to honor the dead.

The following images represent some of the finest, if not underappreciated, works of art that exist not in a museum or private collection but in public for all to see.

Some monuments or designs were created by well-known sculptures and artists of their day while others stand as a testament to the many nameless artists who made a living through death.

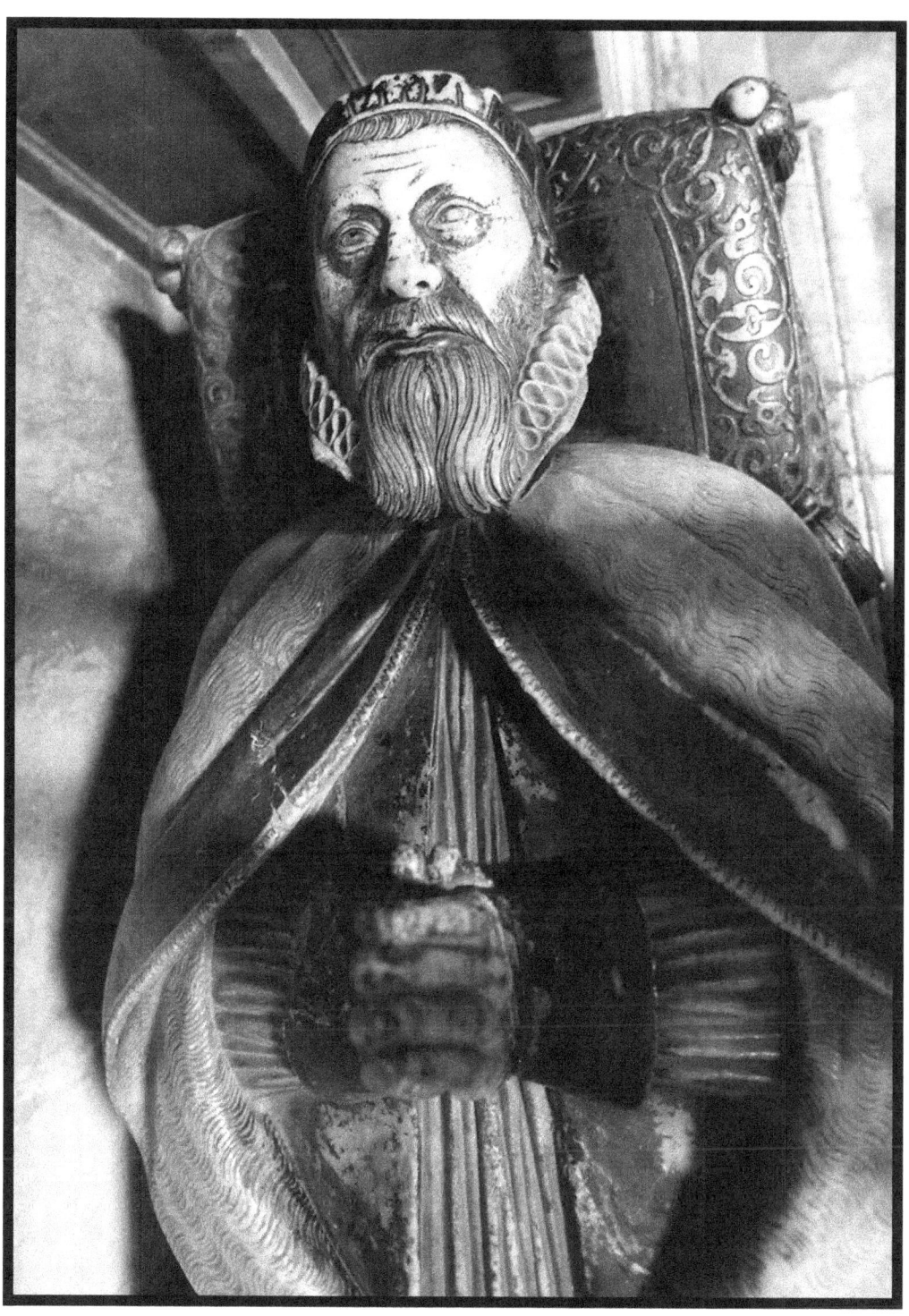

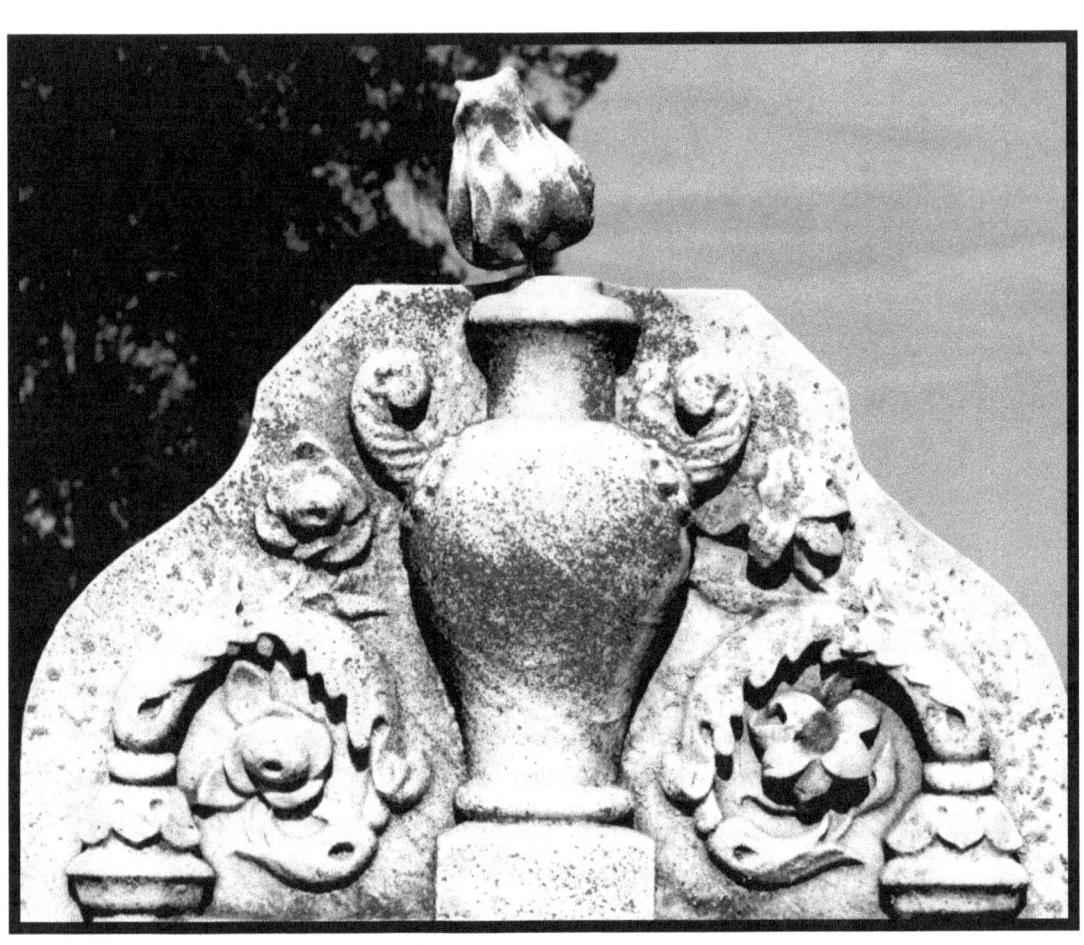

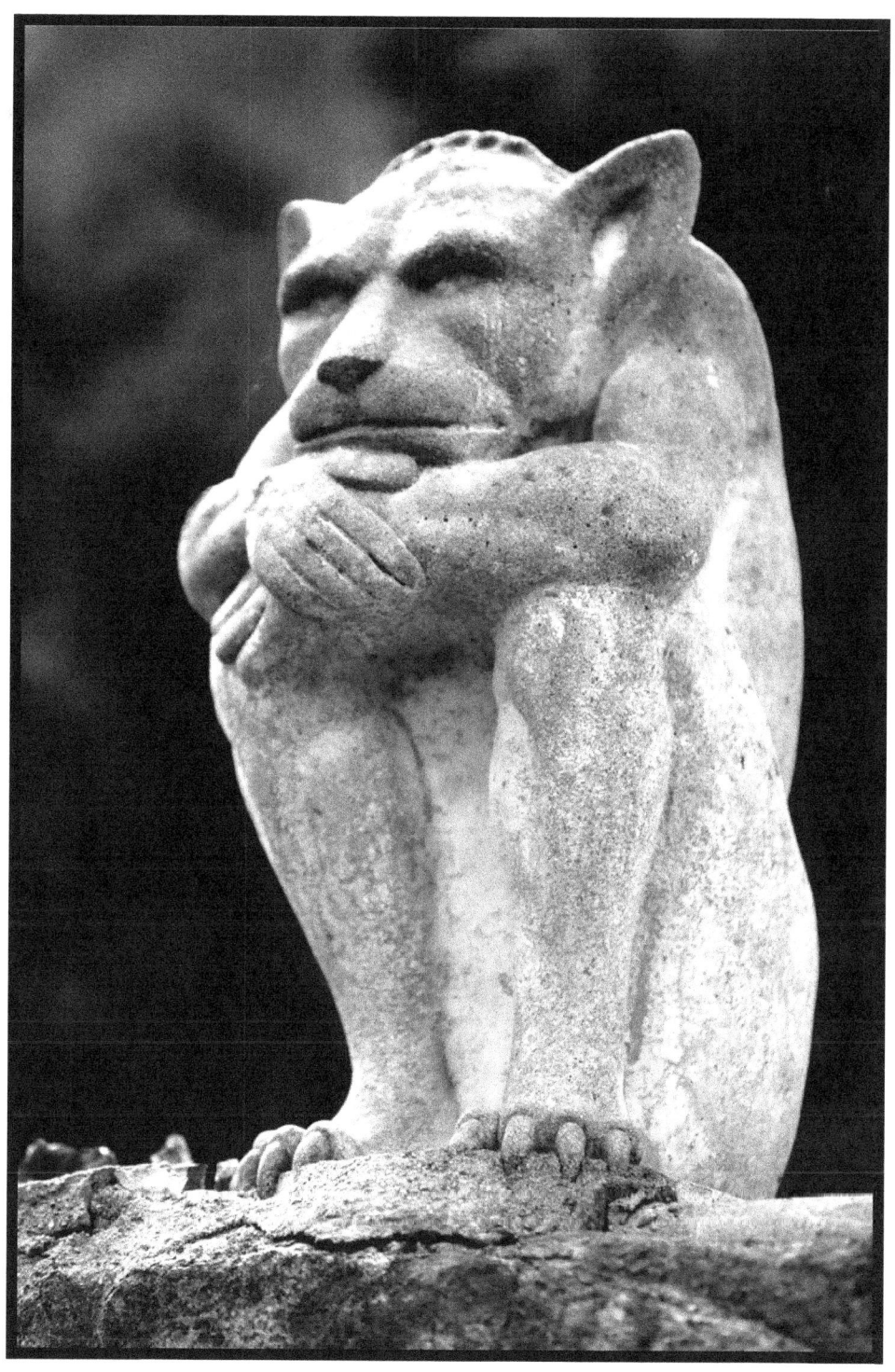

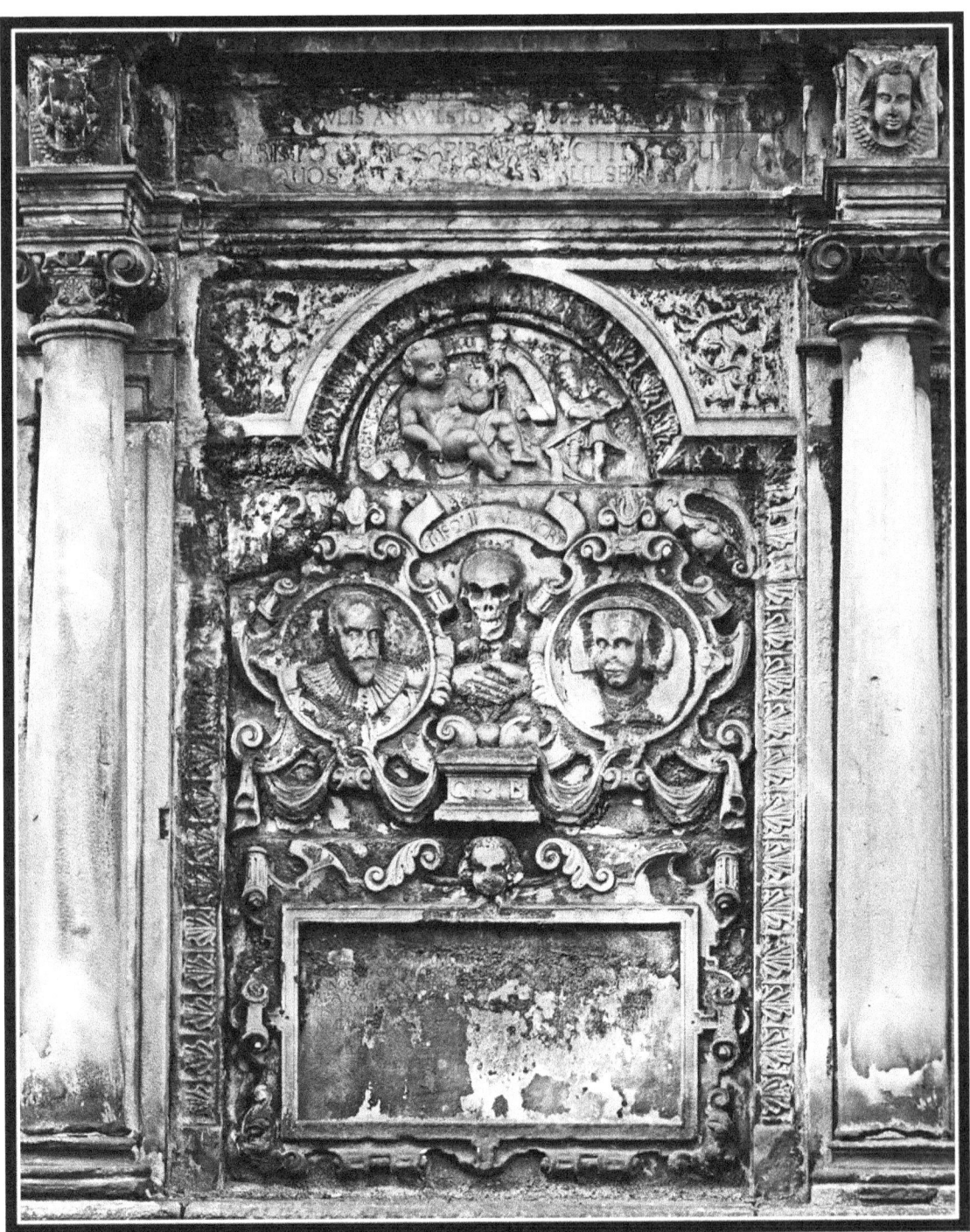

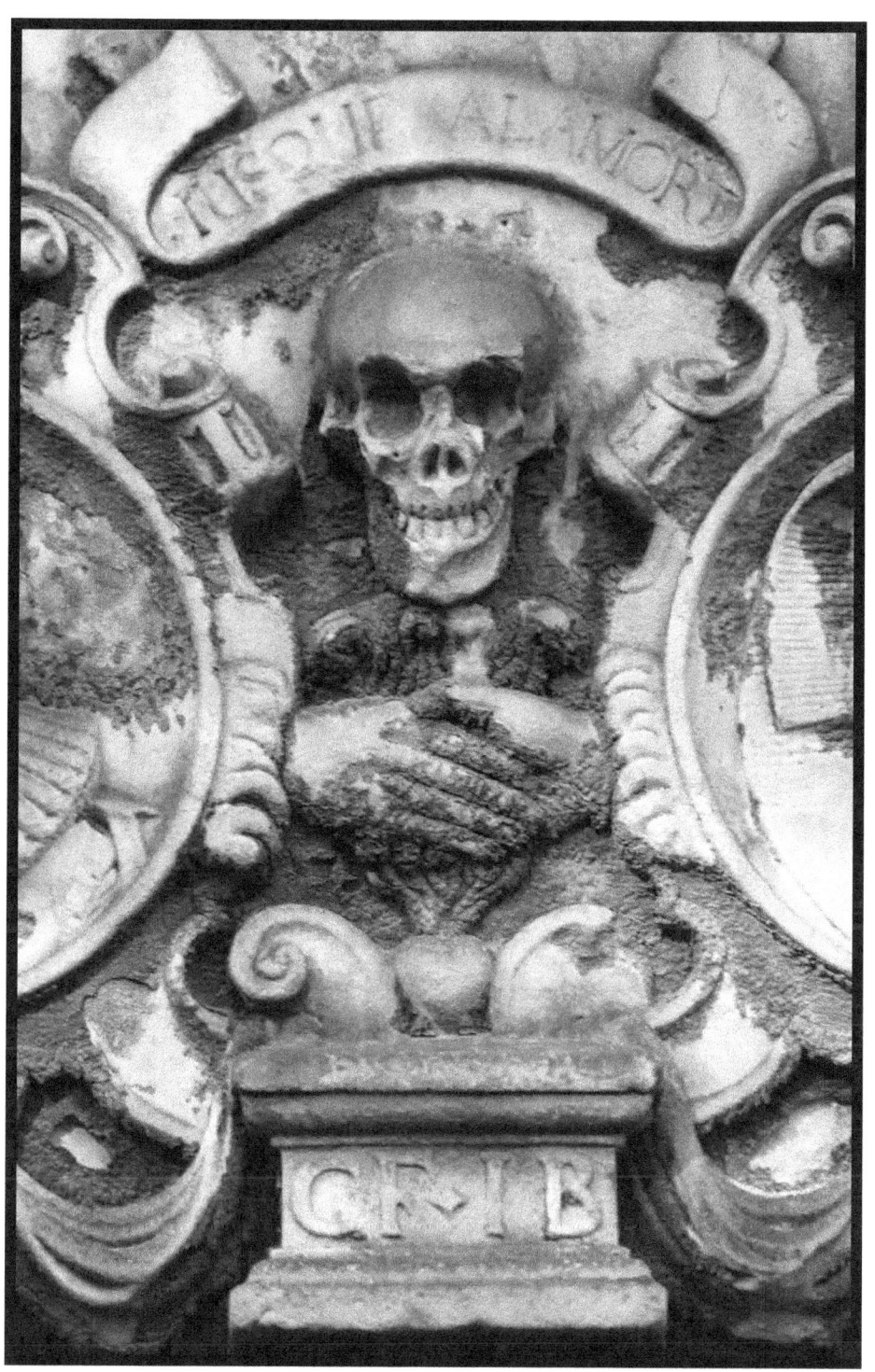

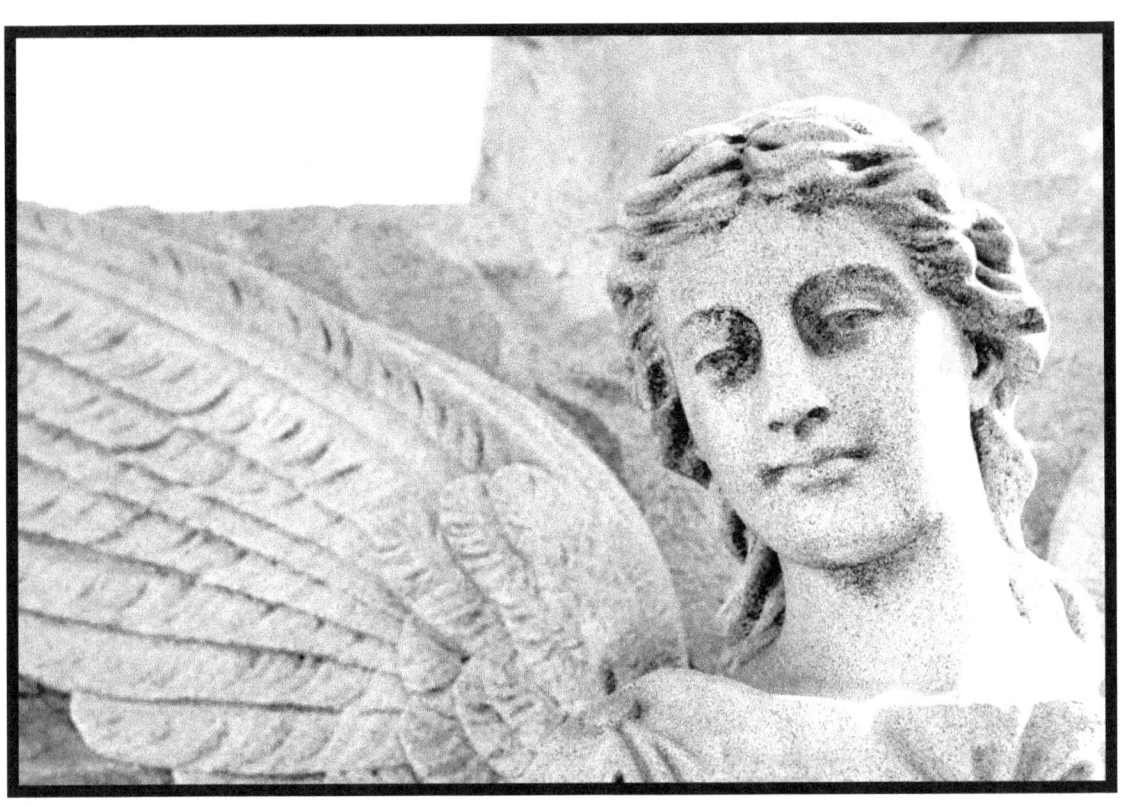

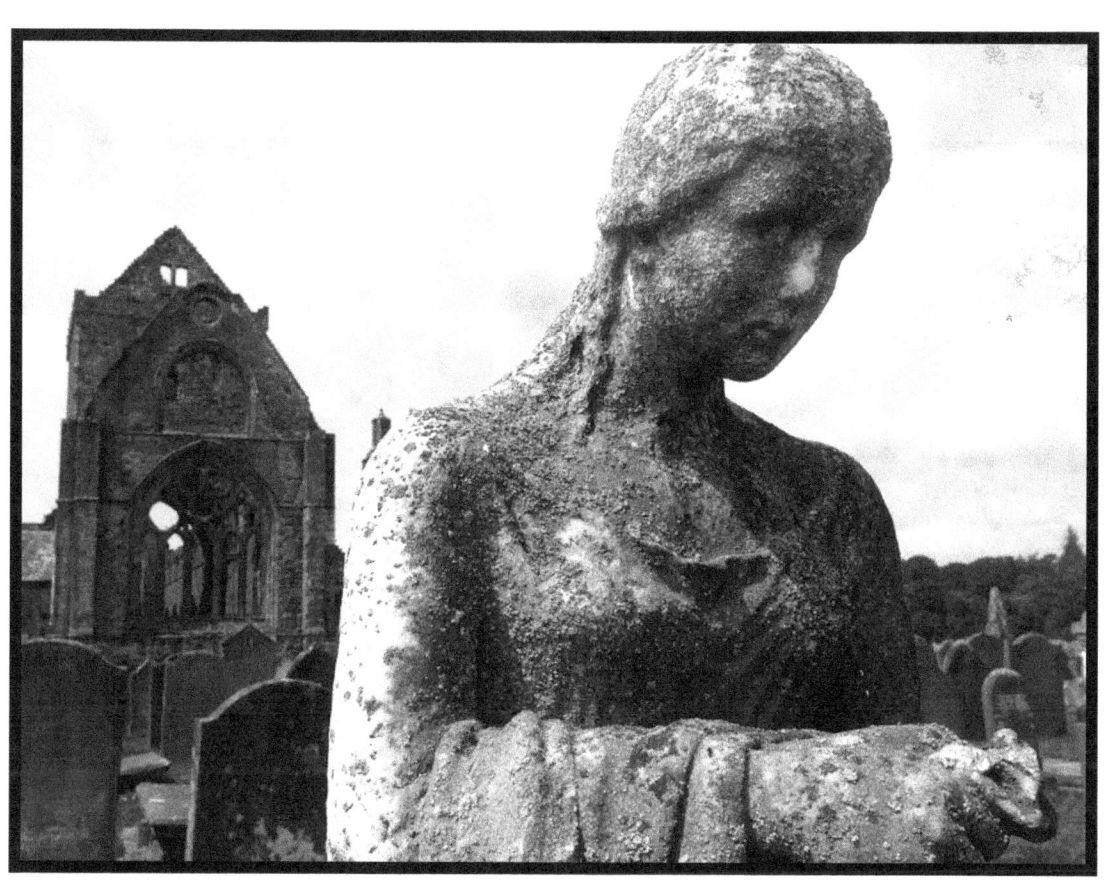

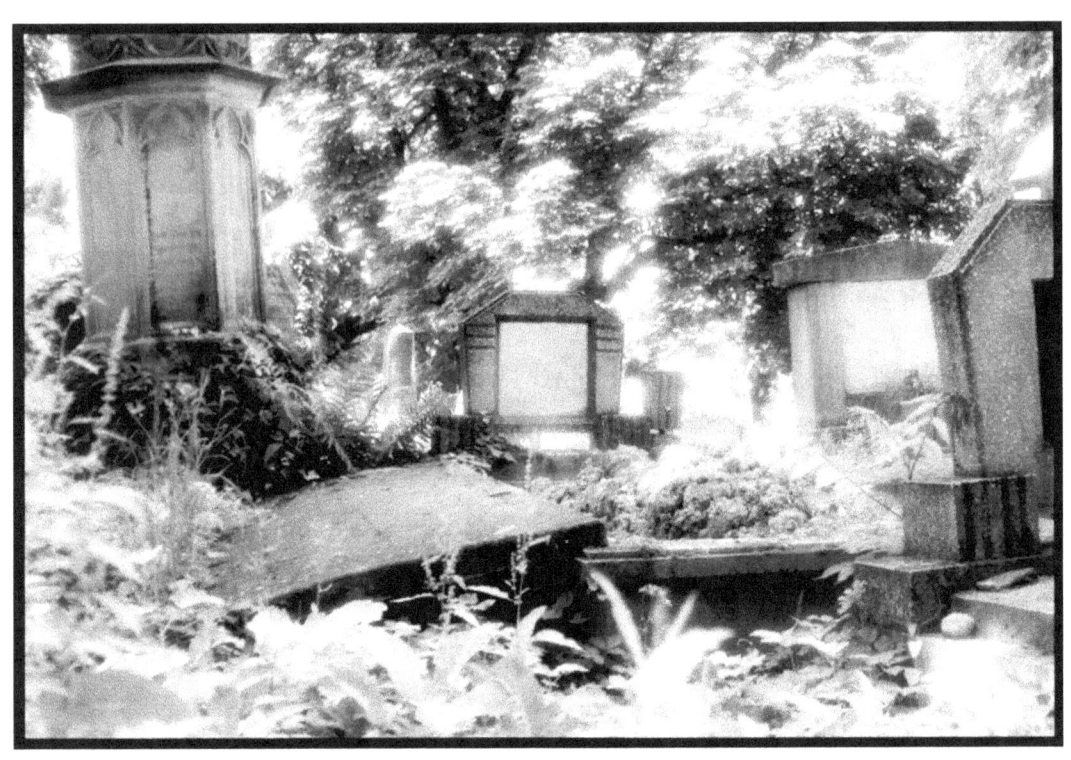

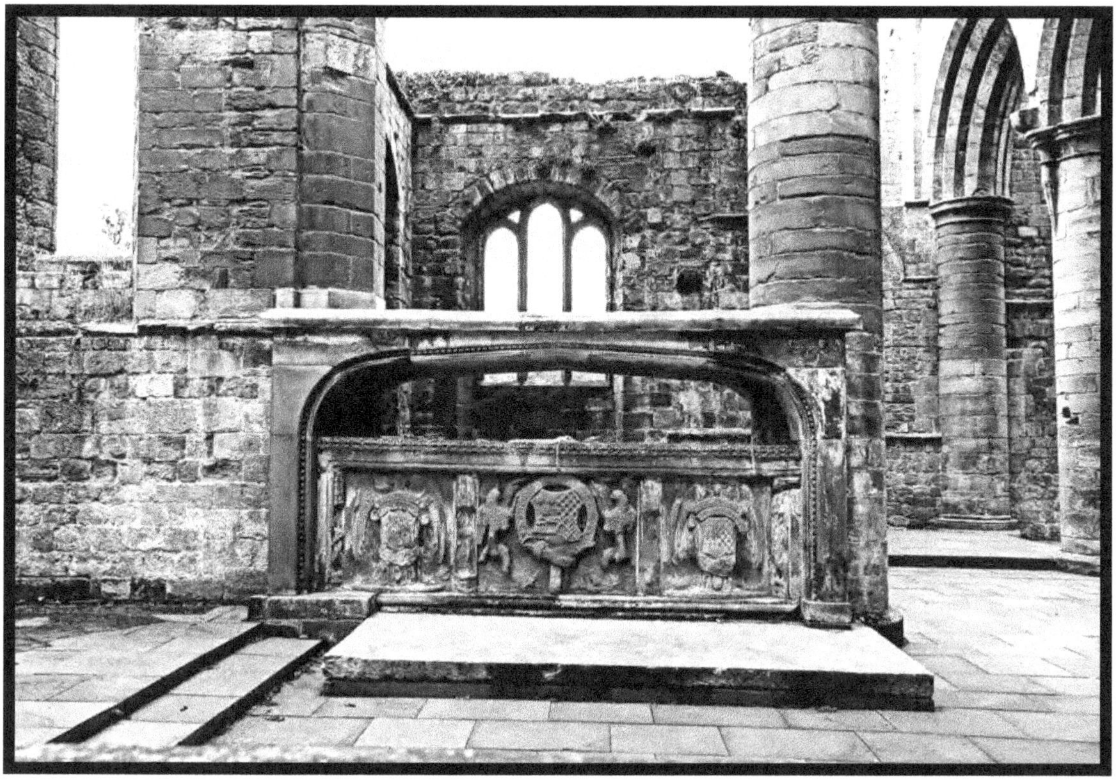

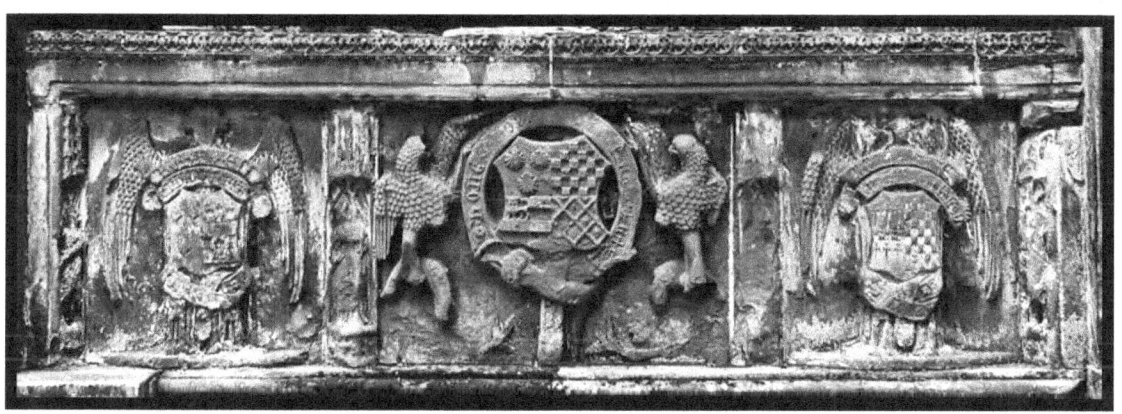

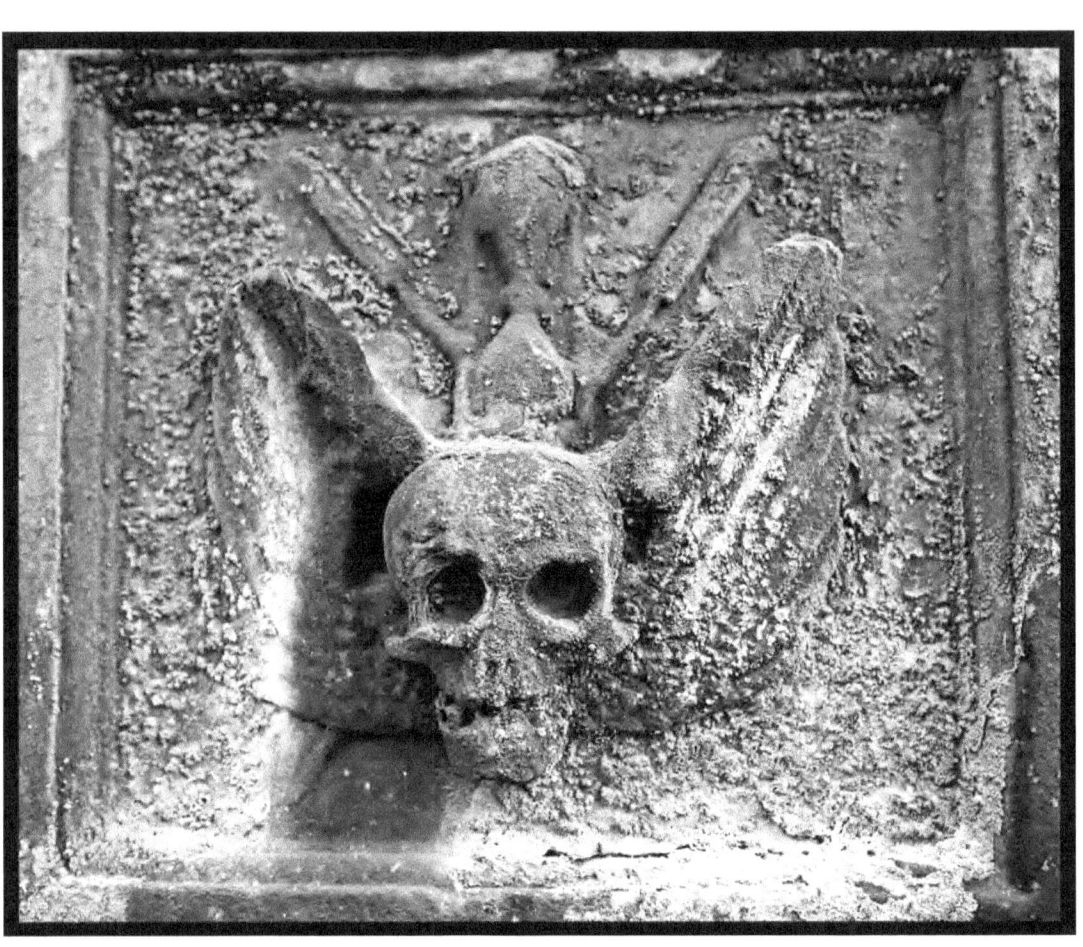

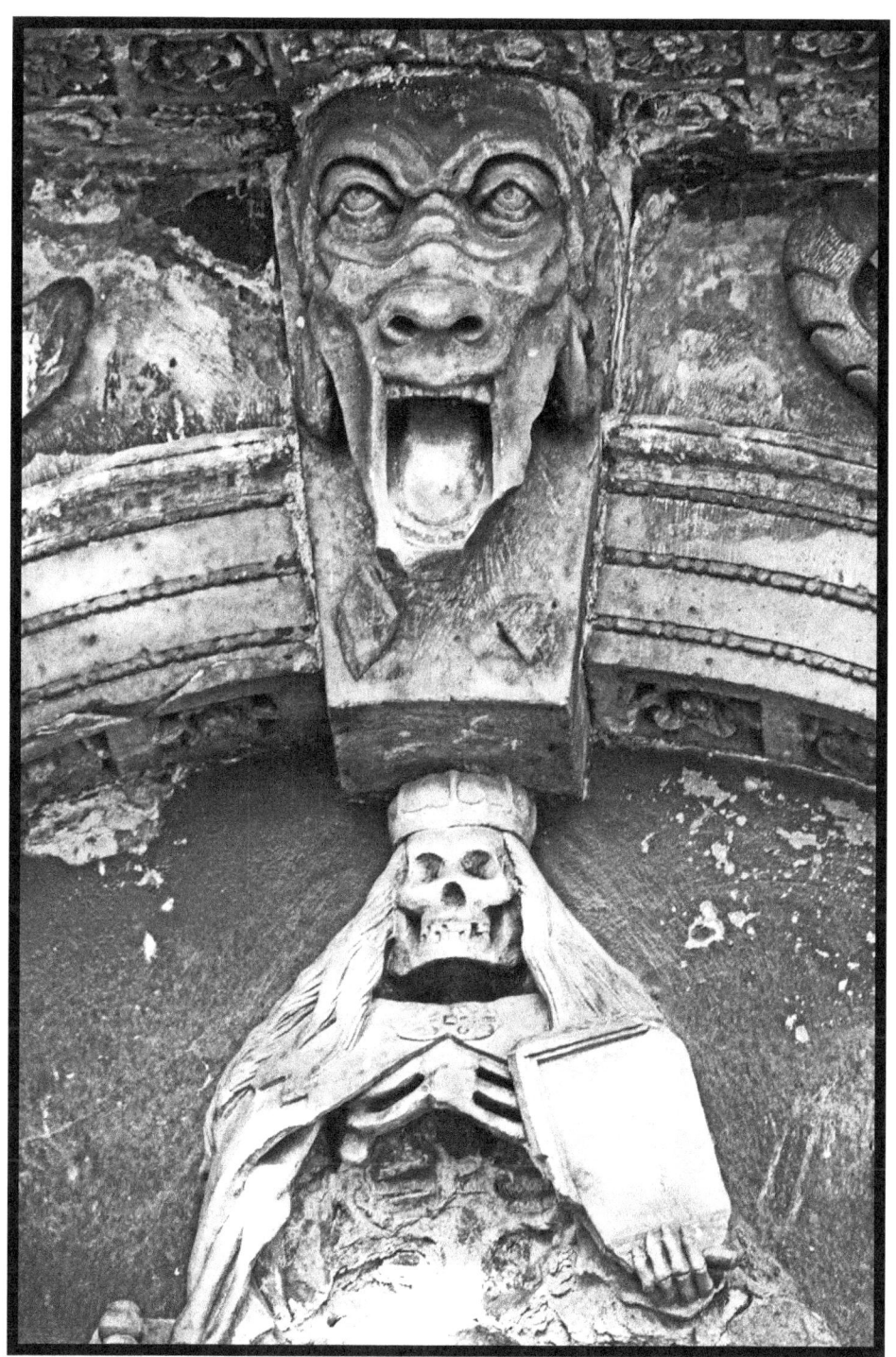

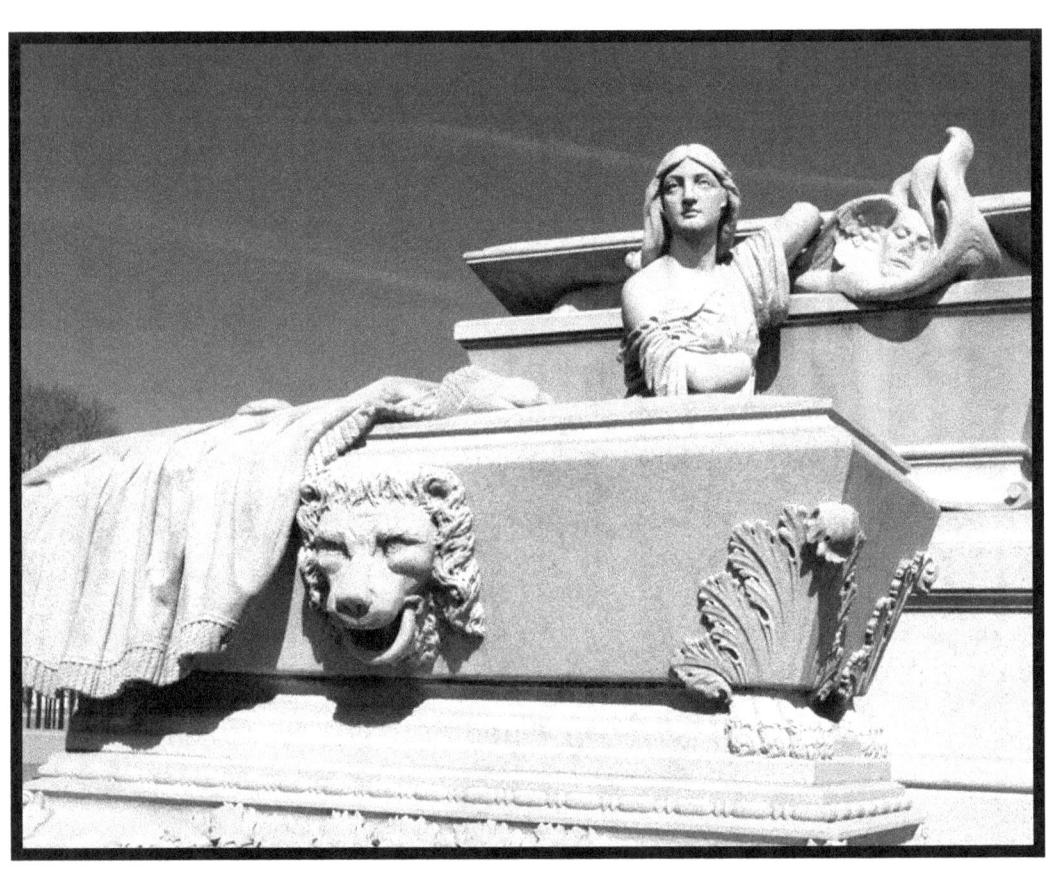

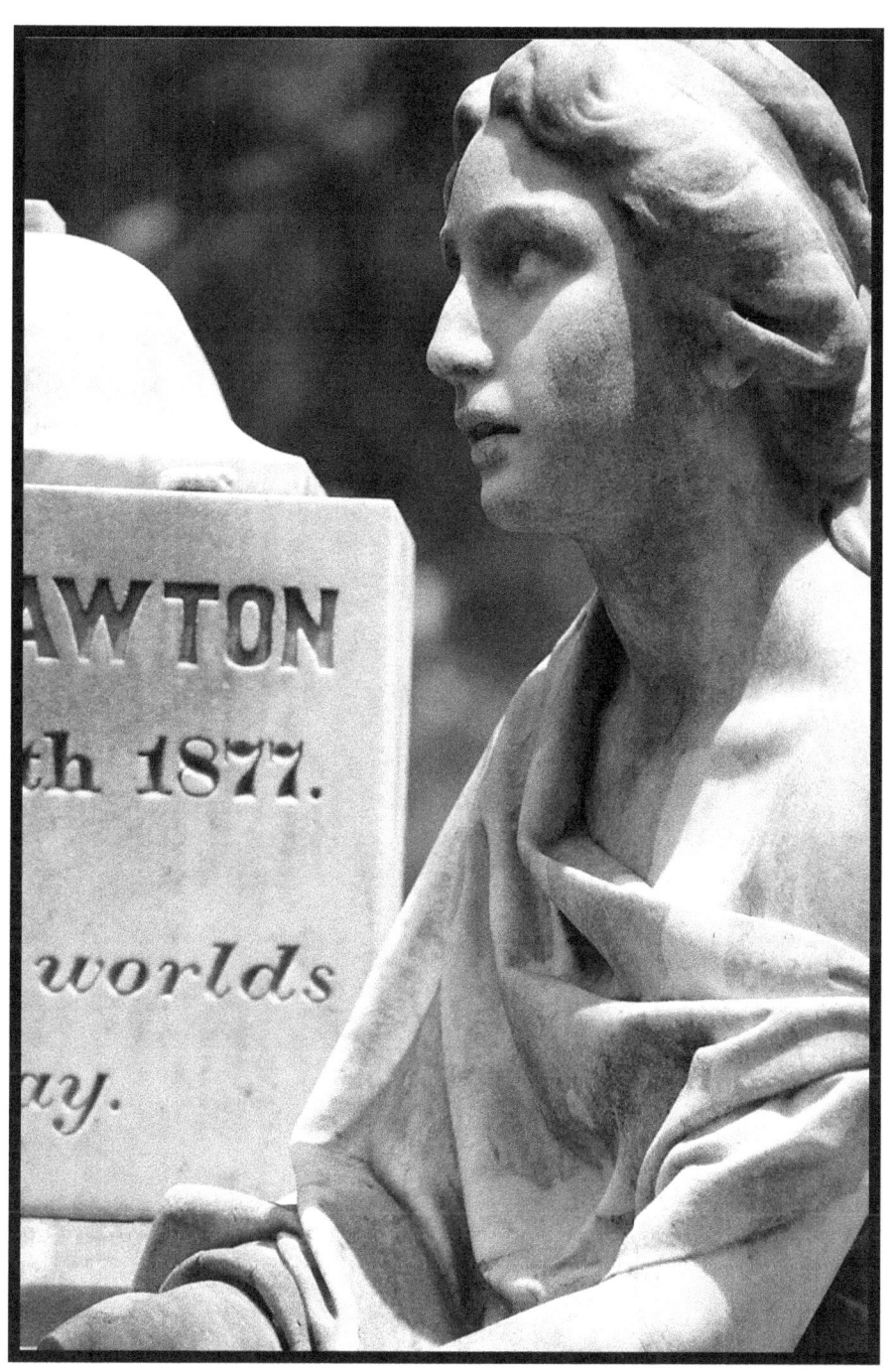

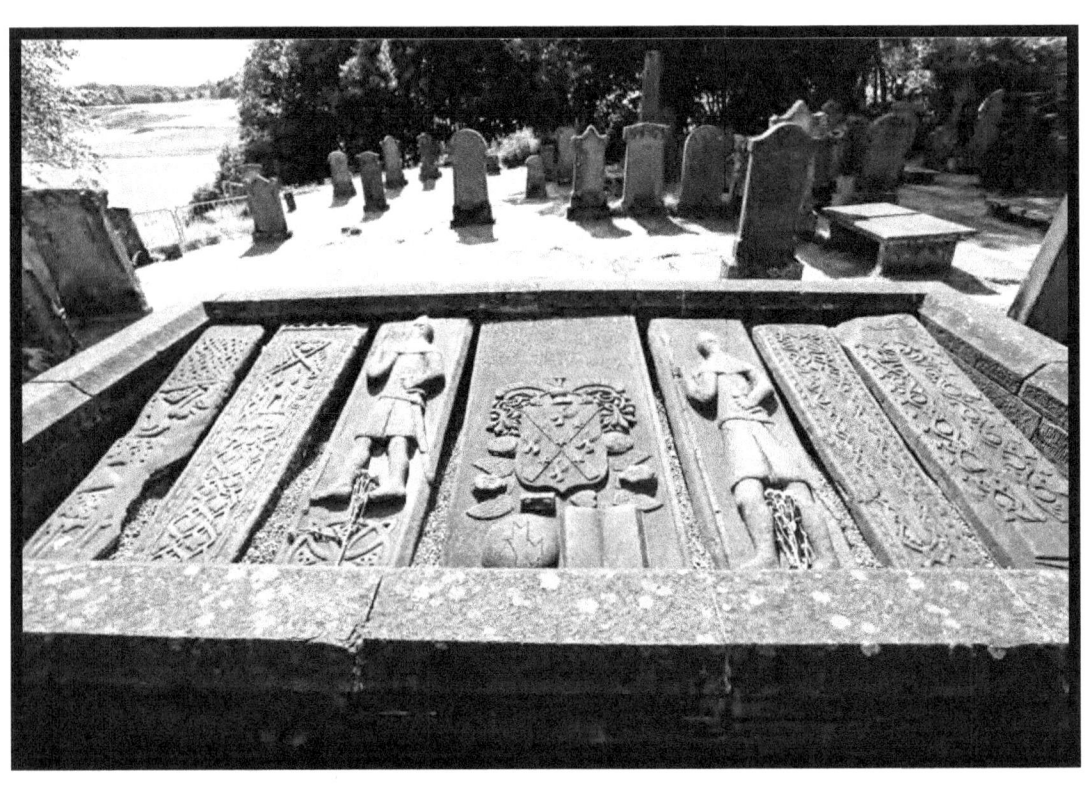

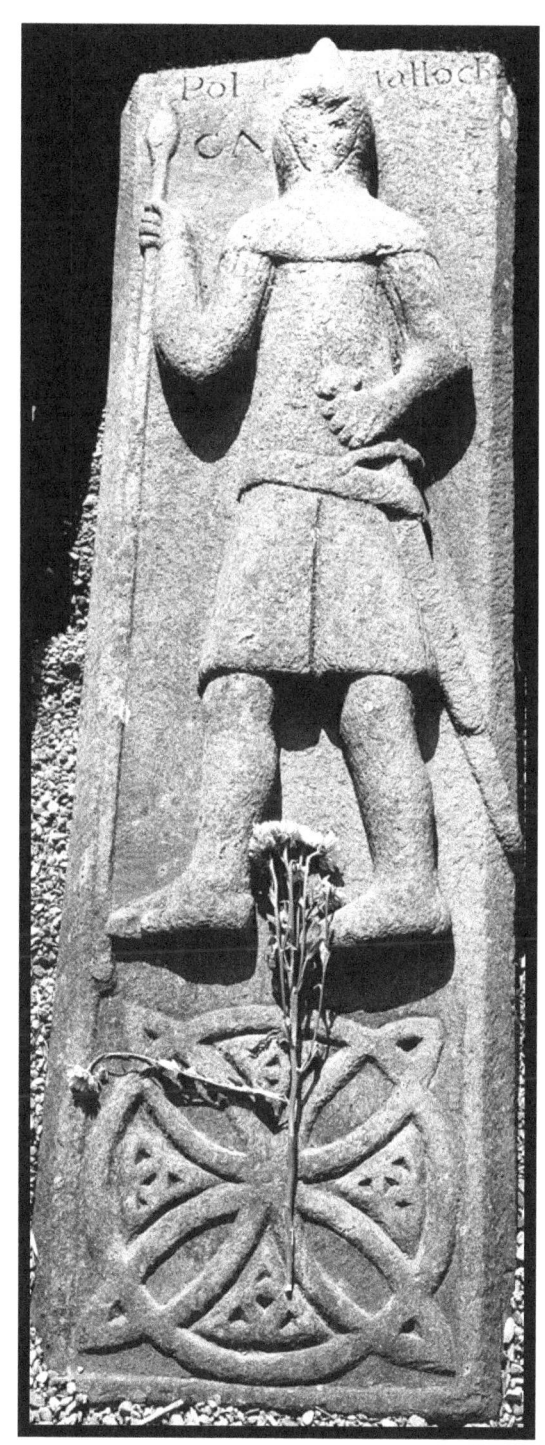

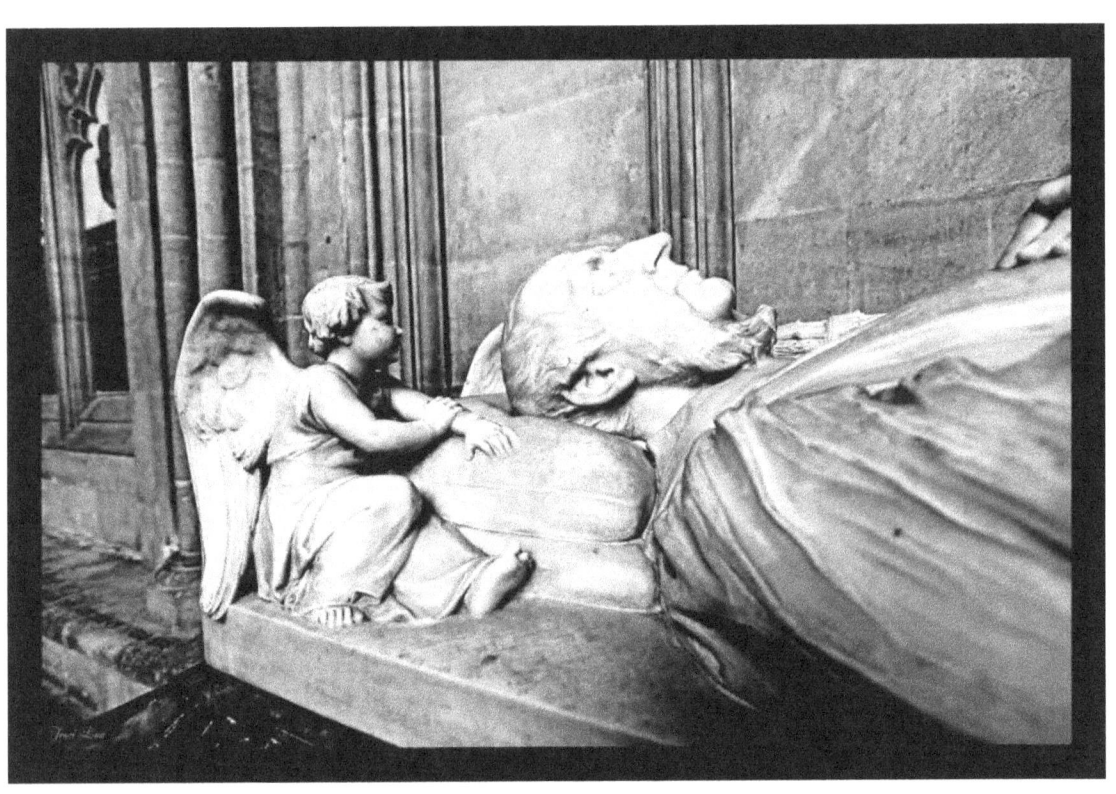

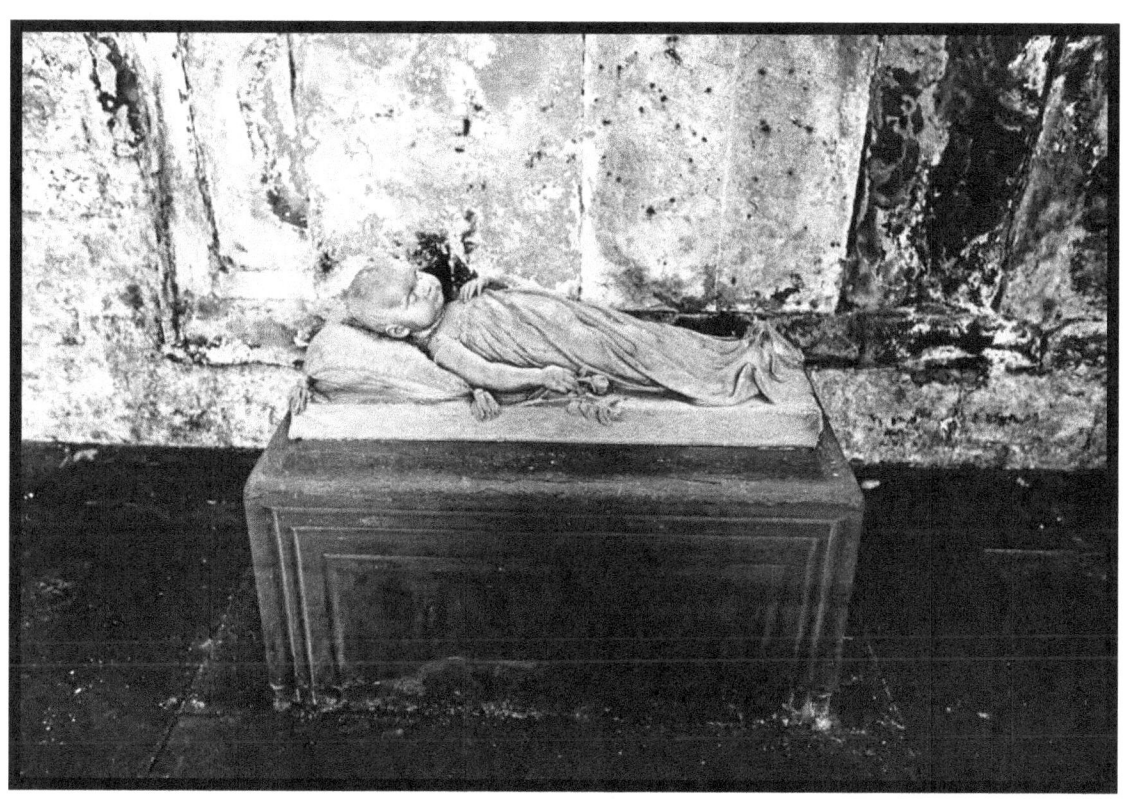

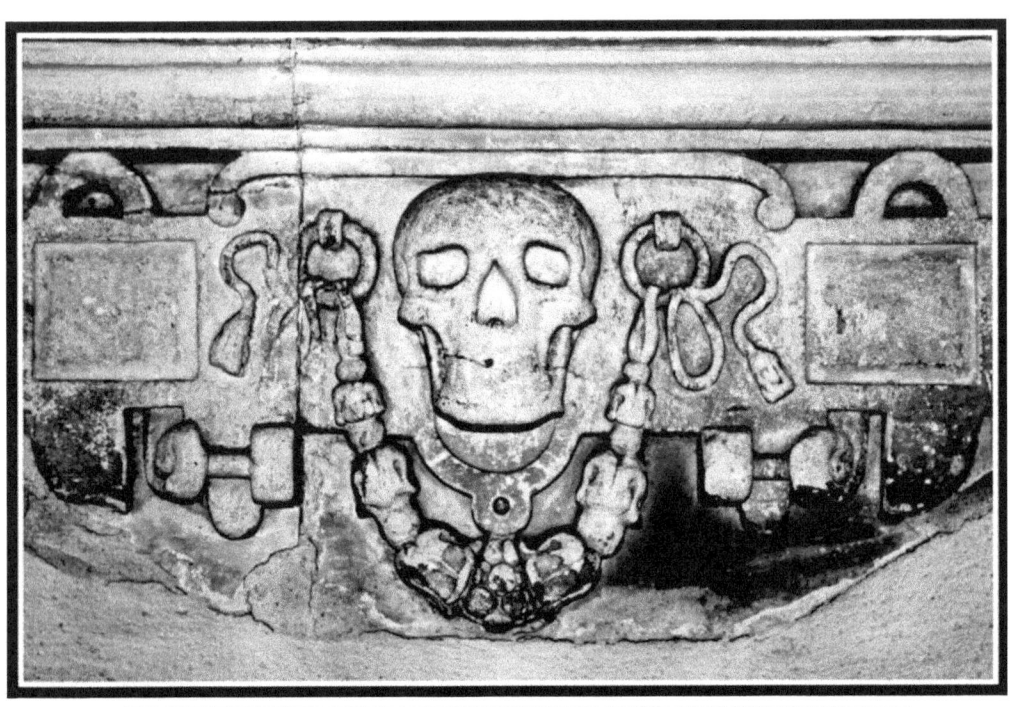

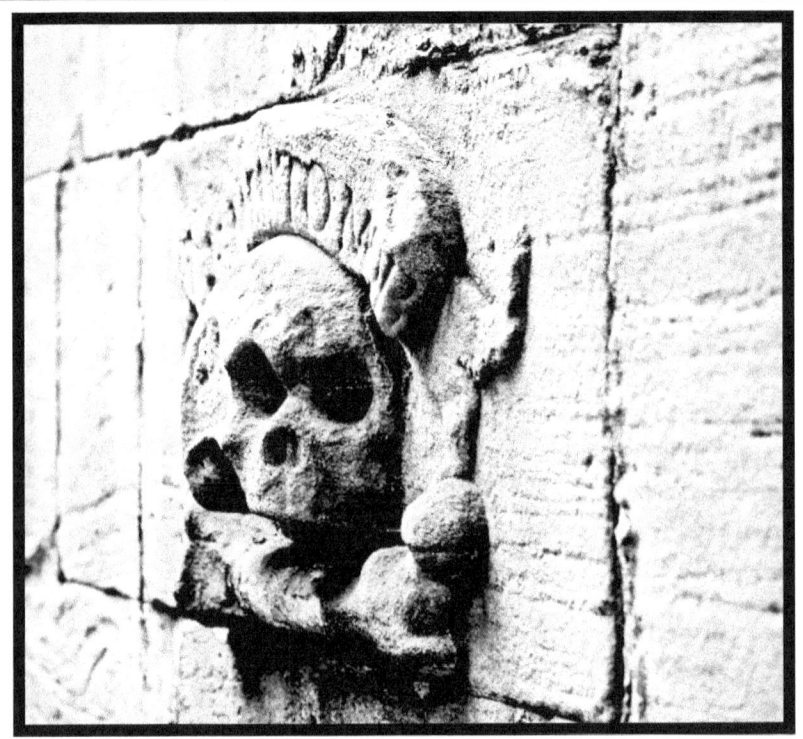

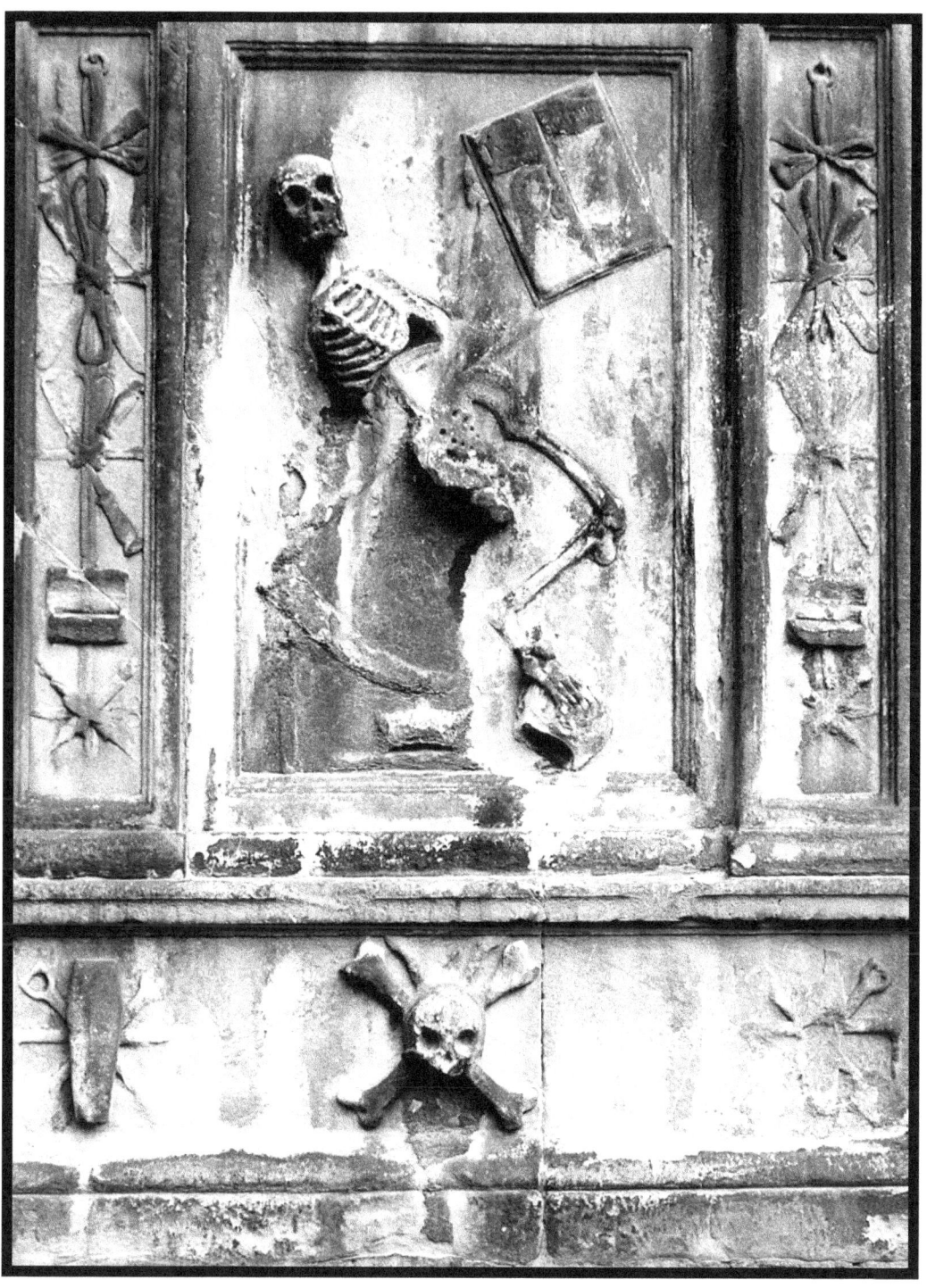

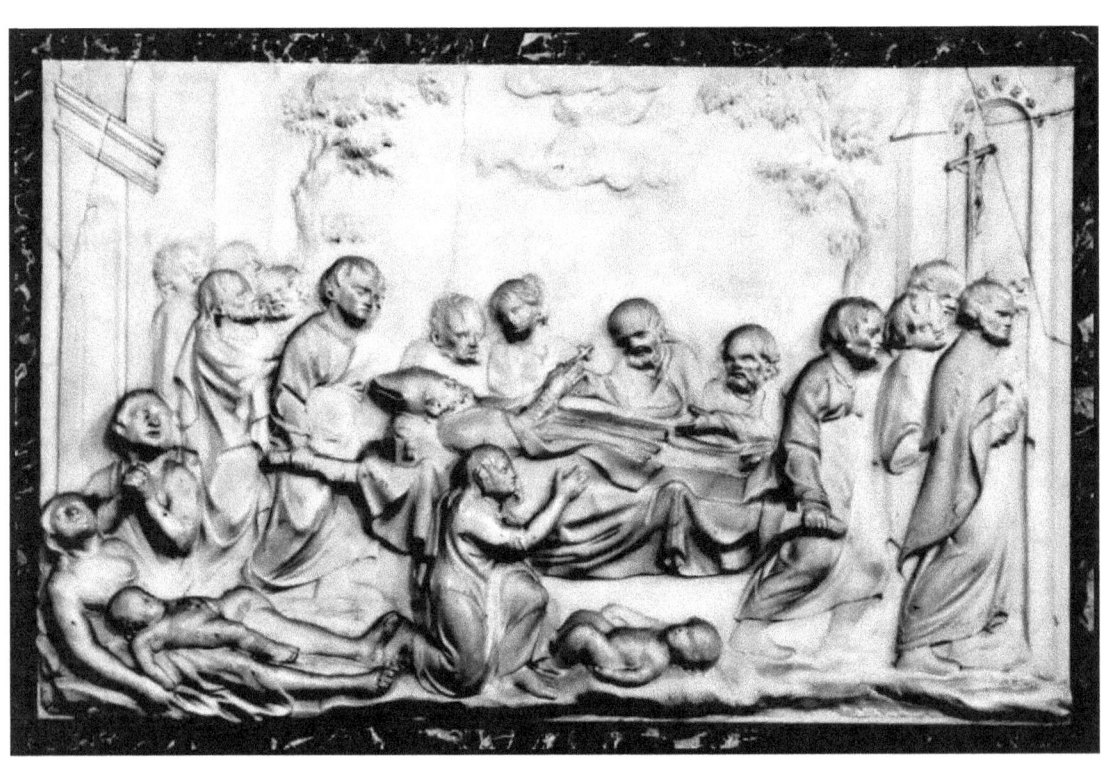

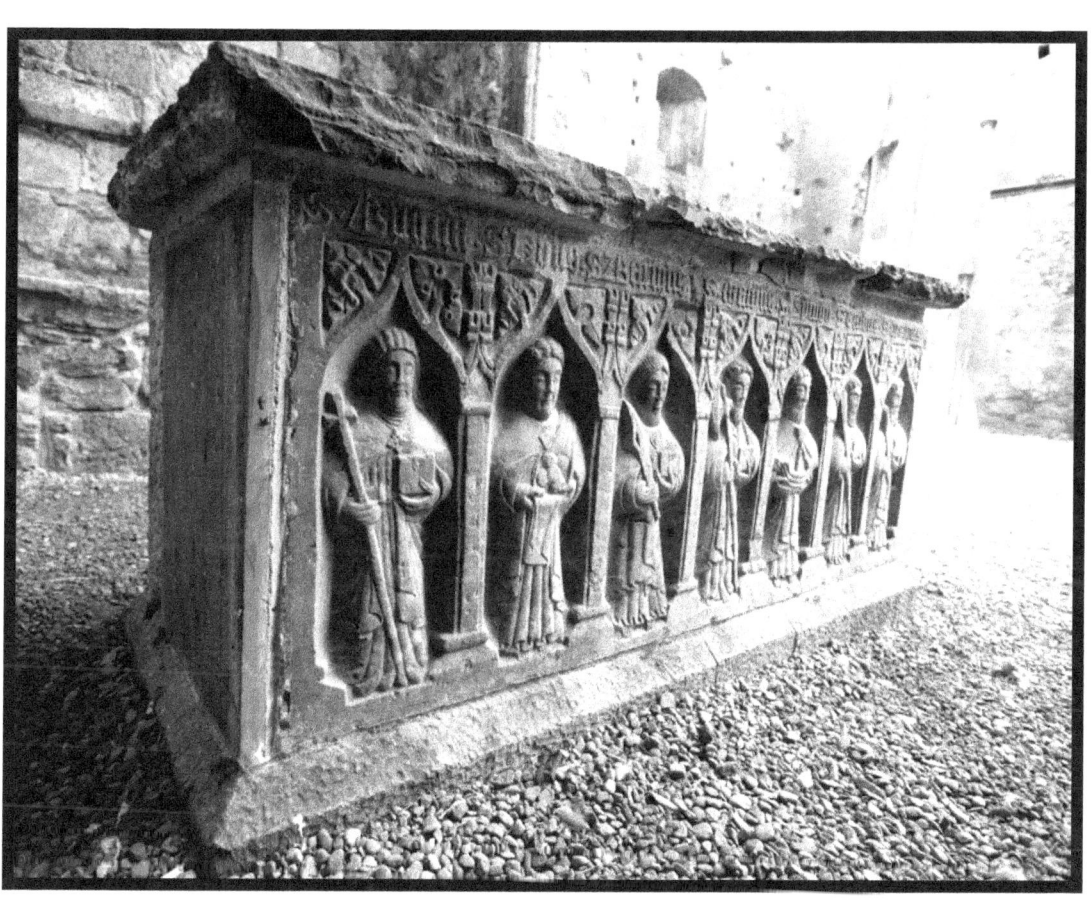

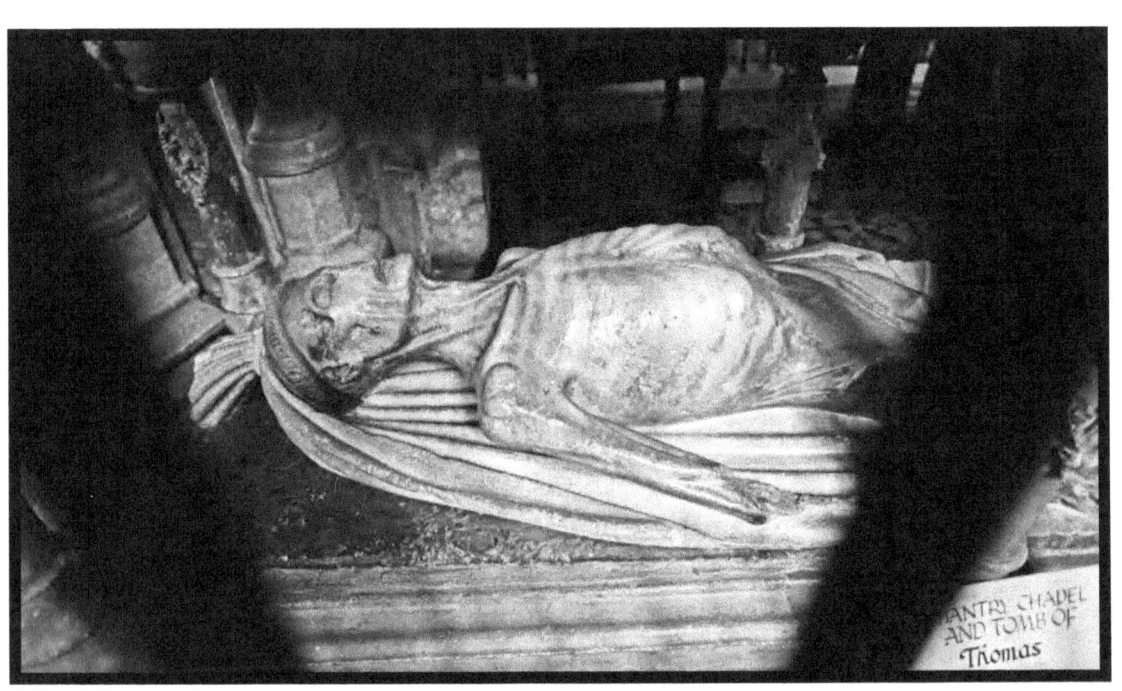

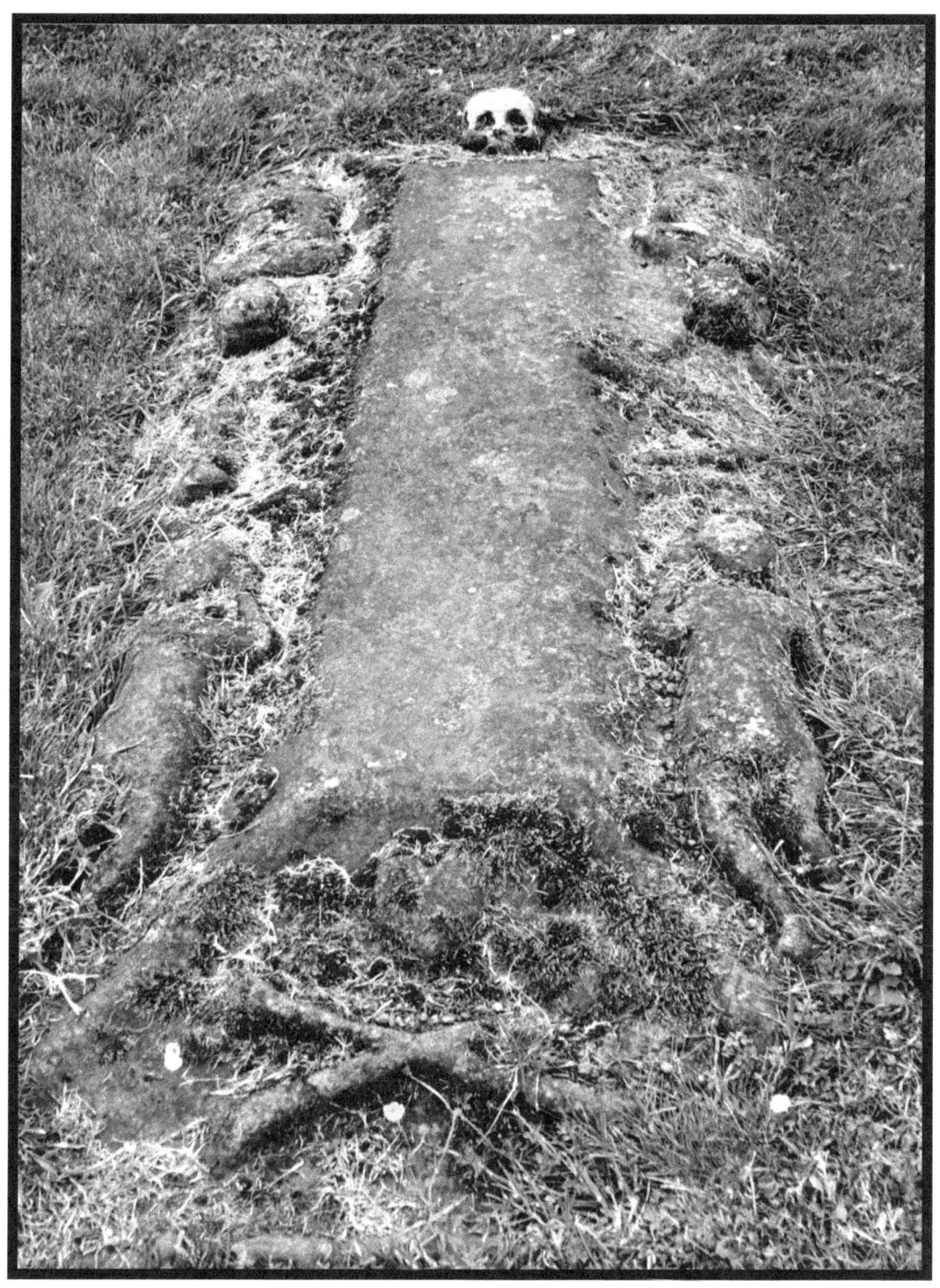

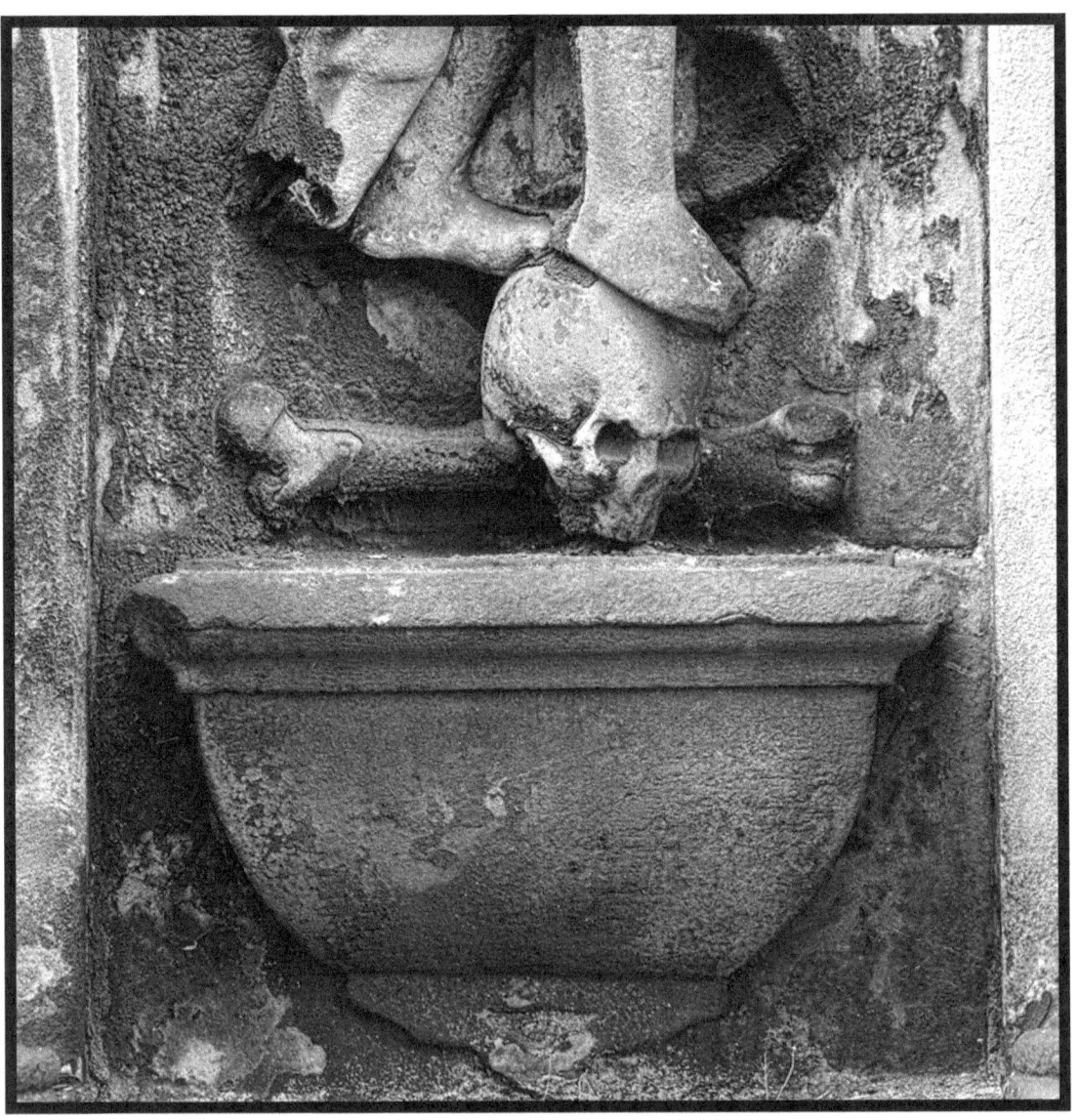

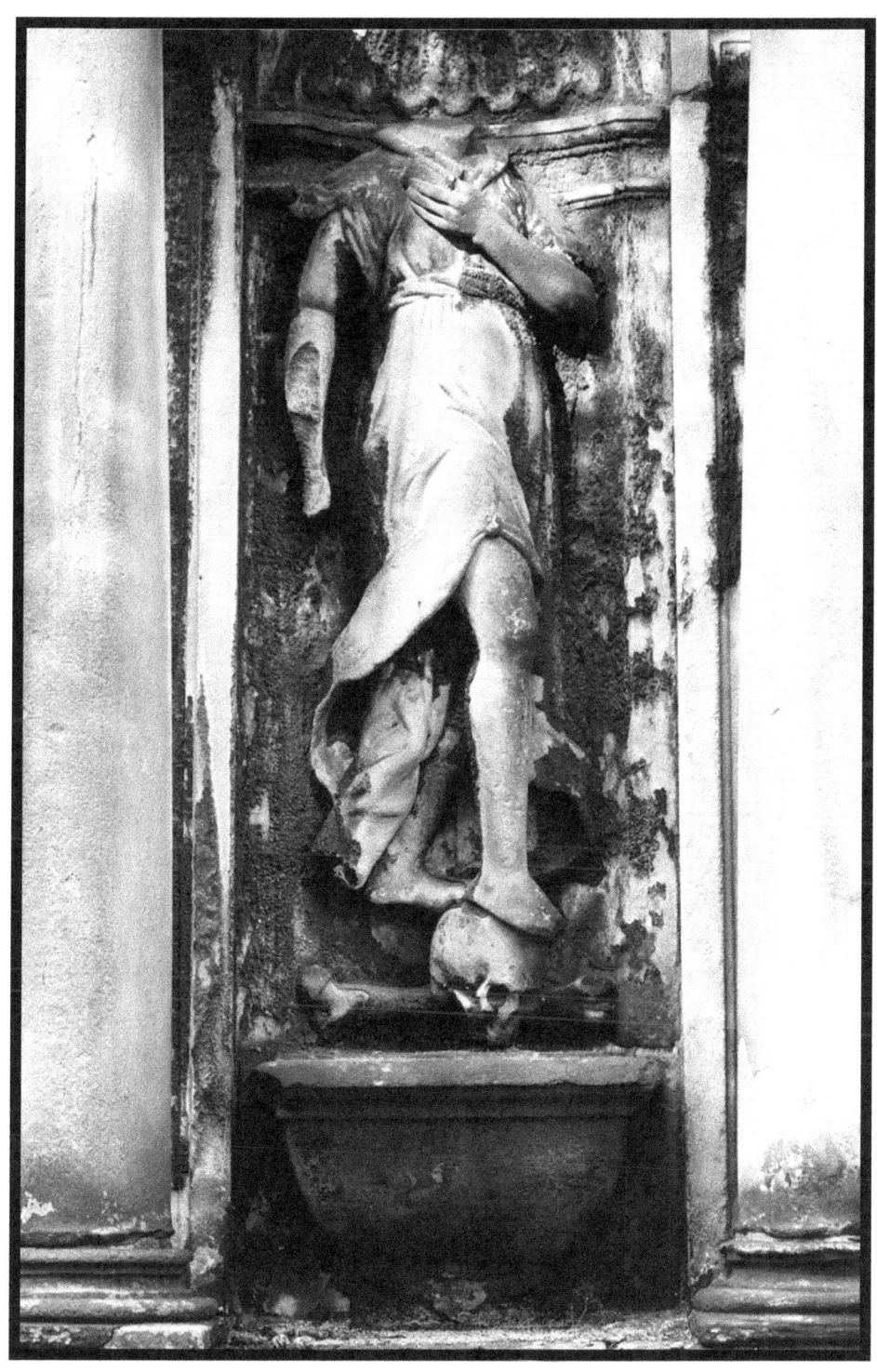

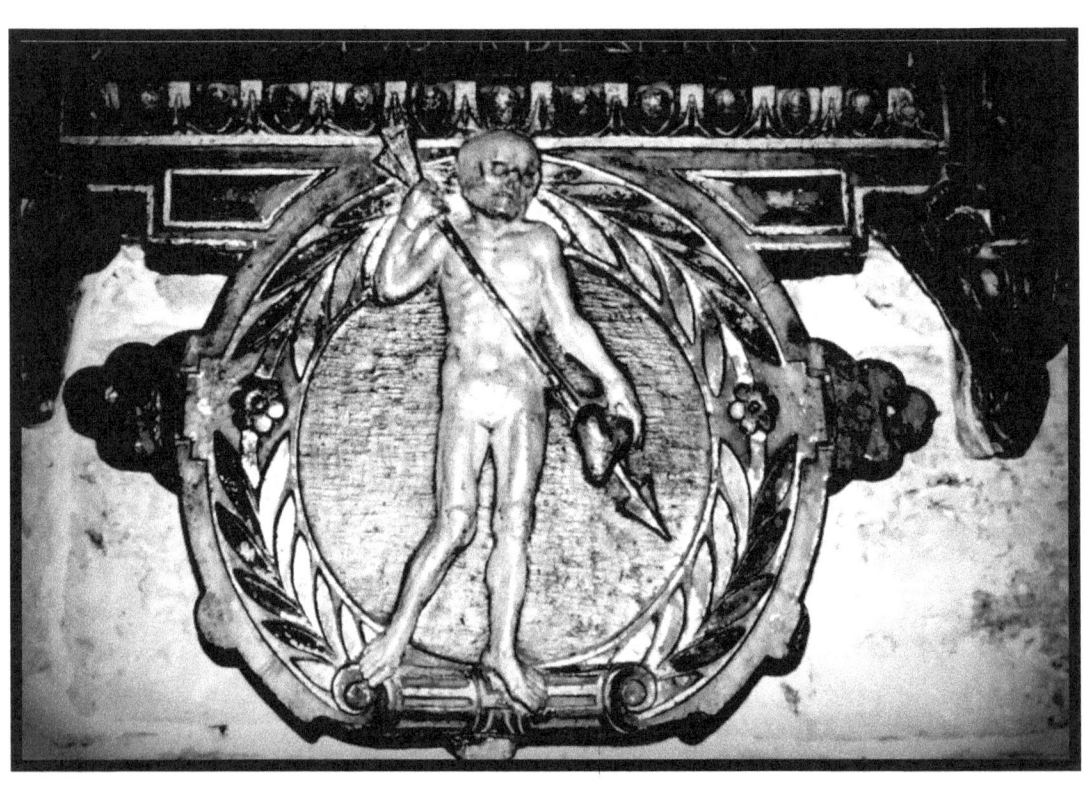

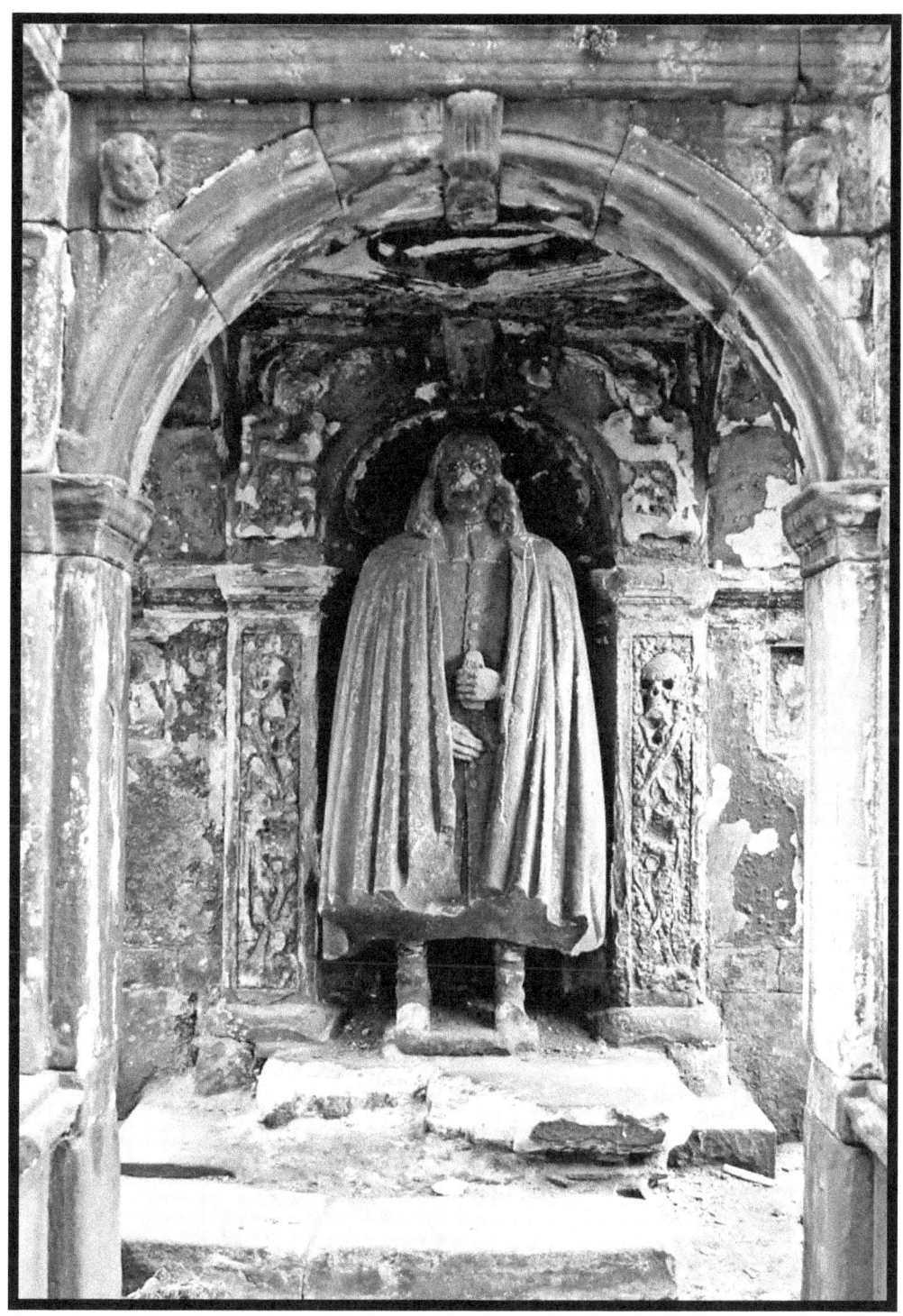

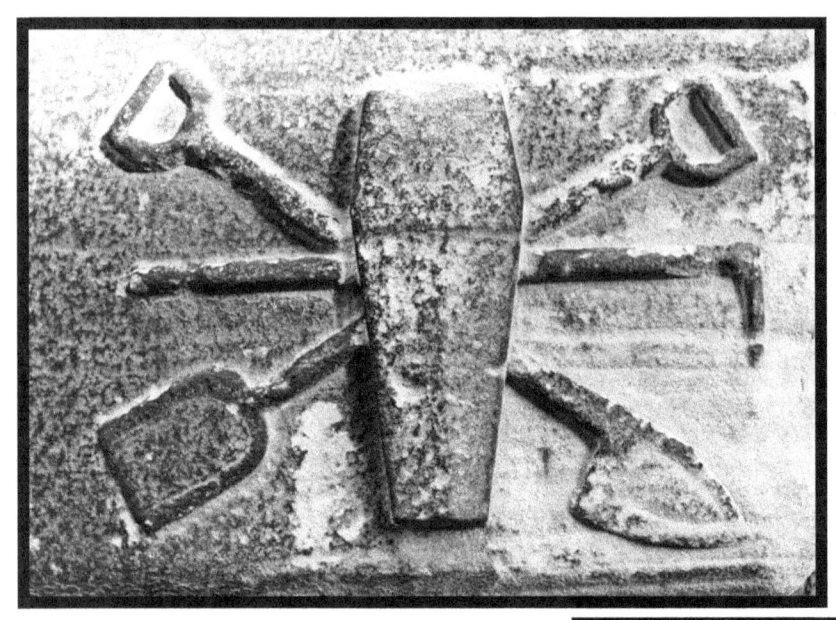

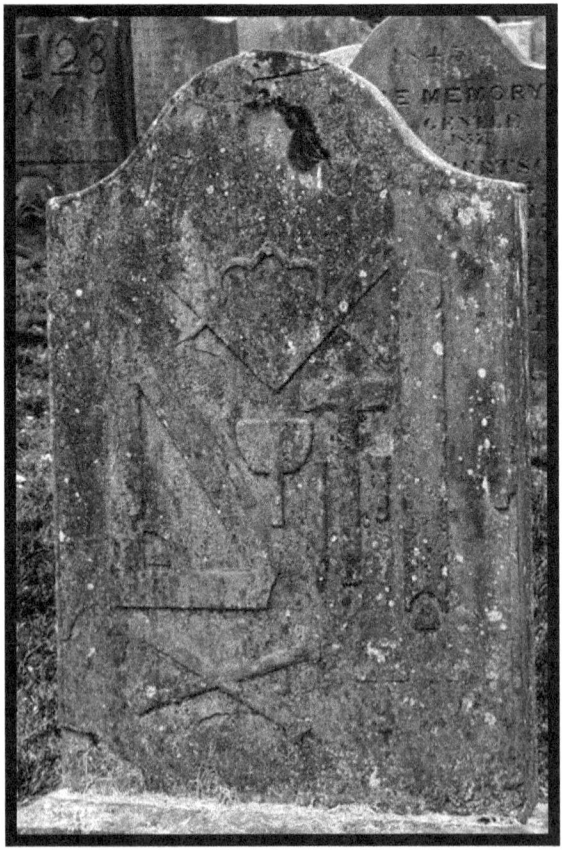

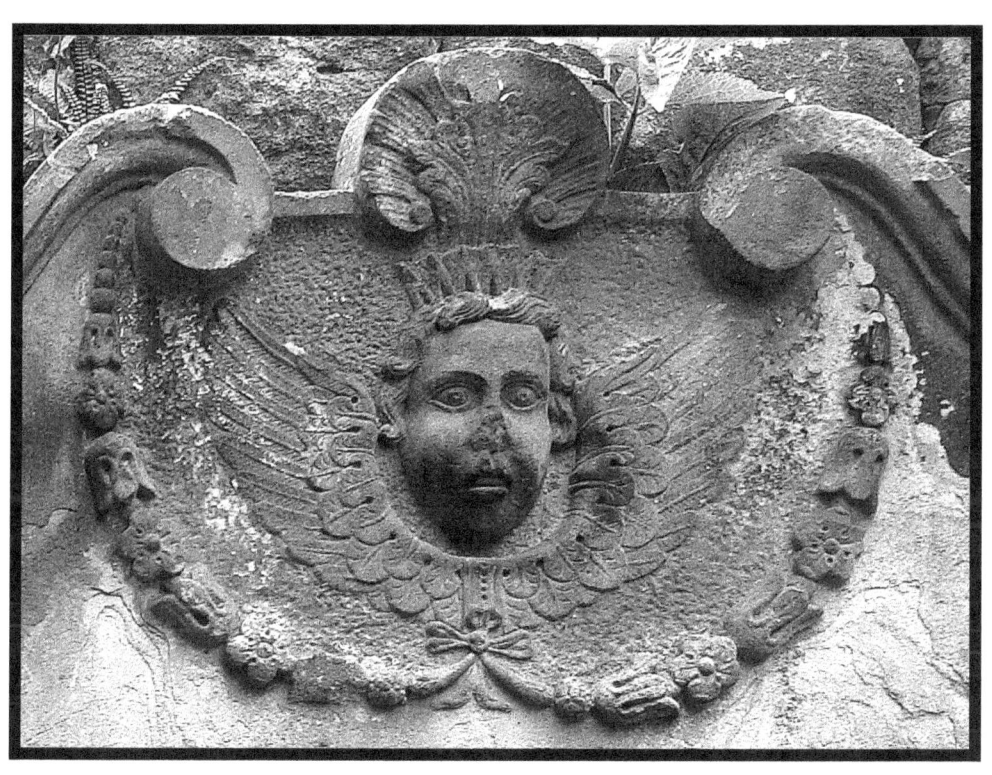

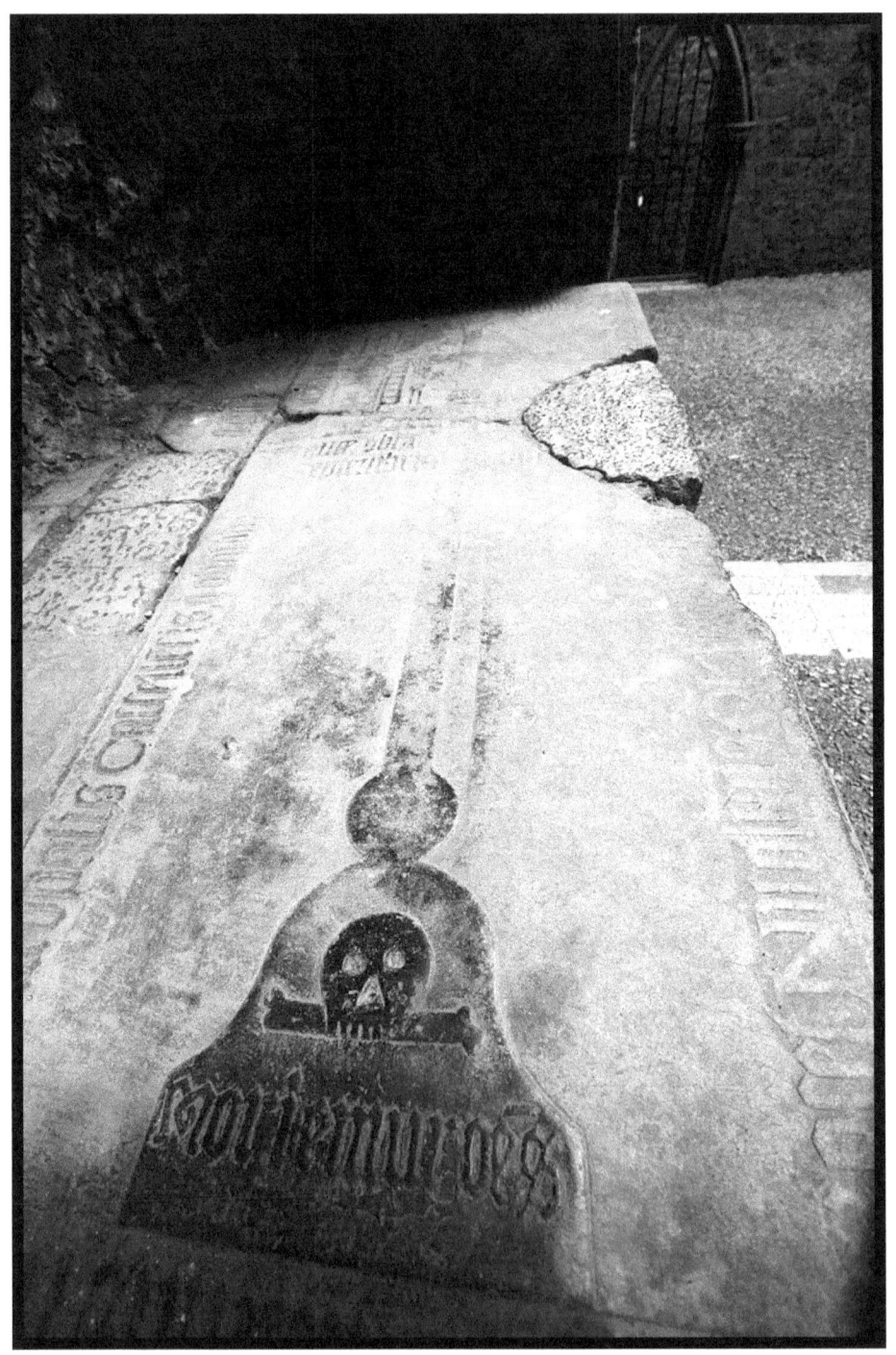

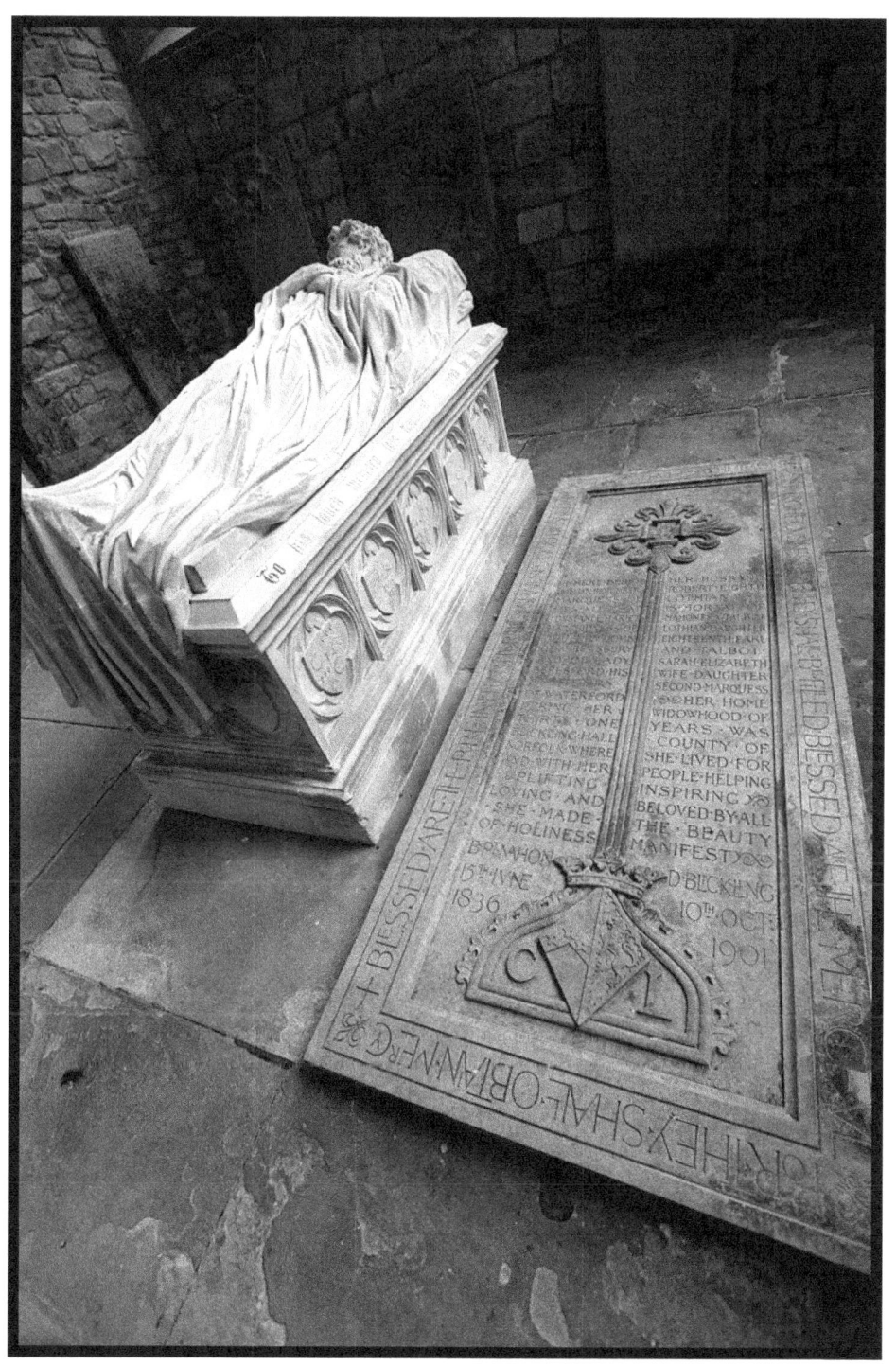

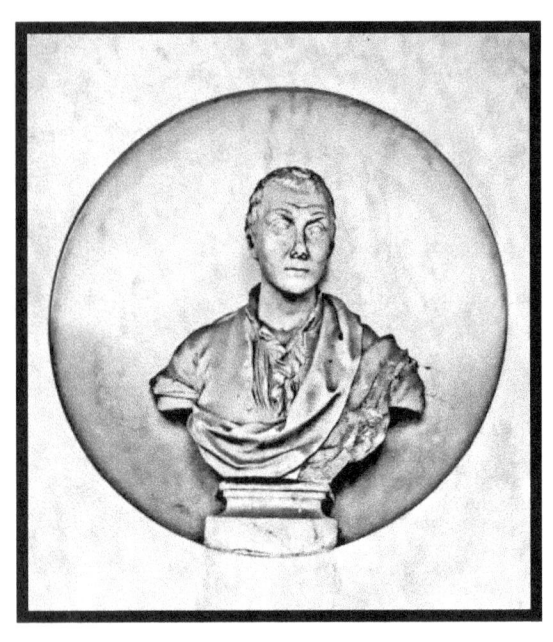

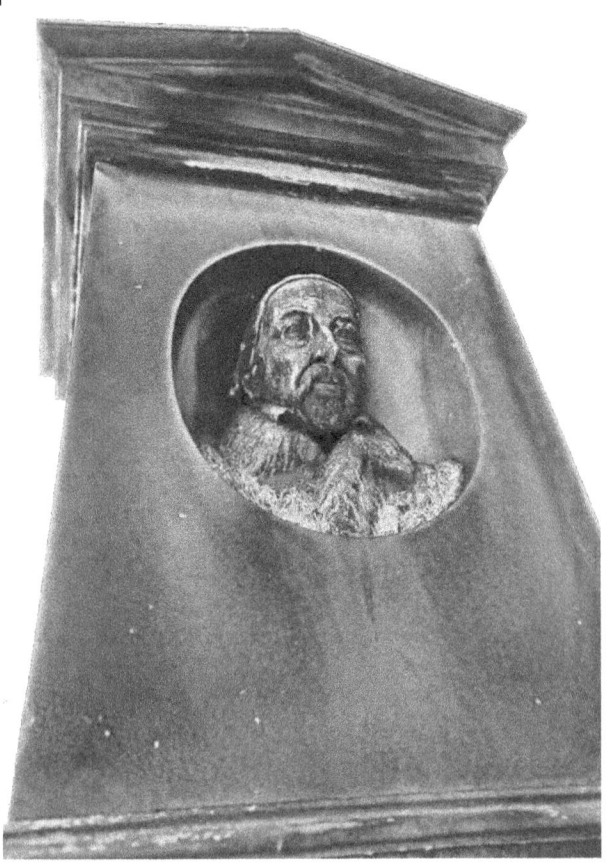

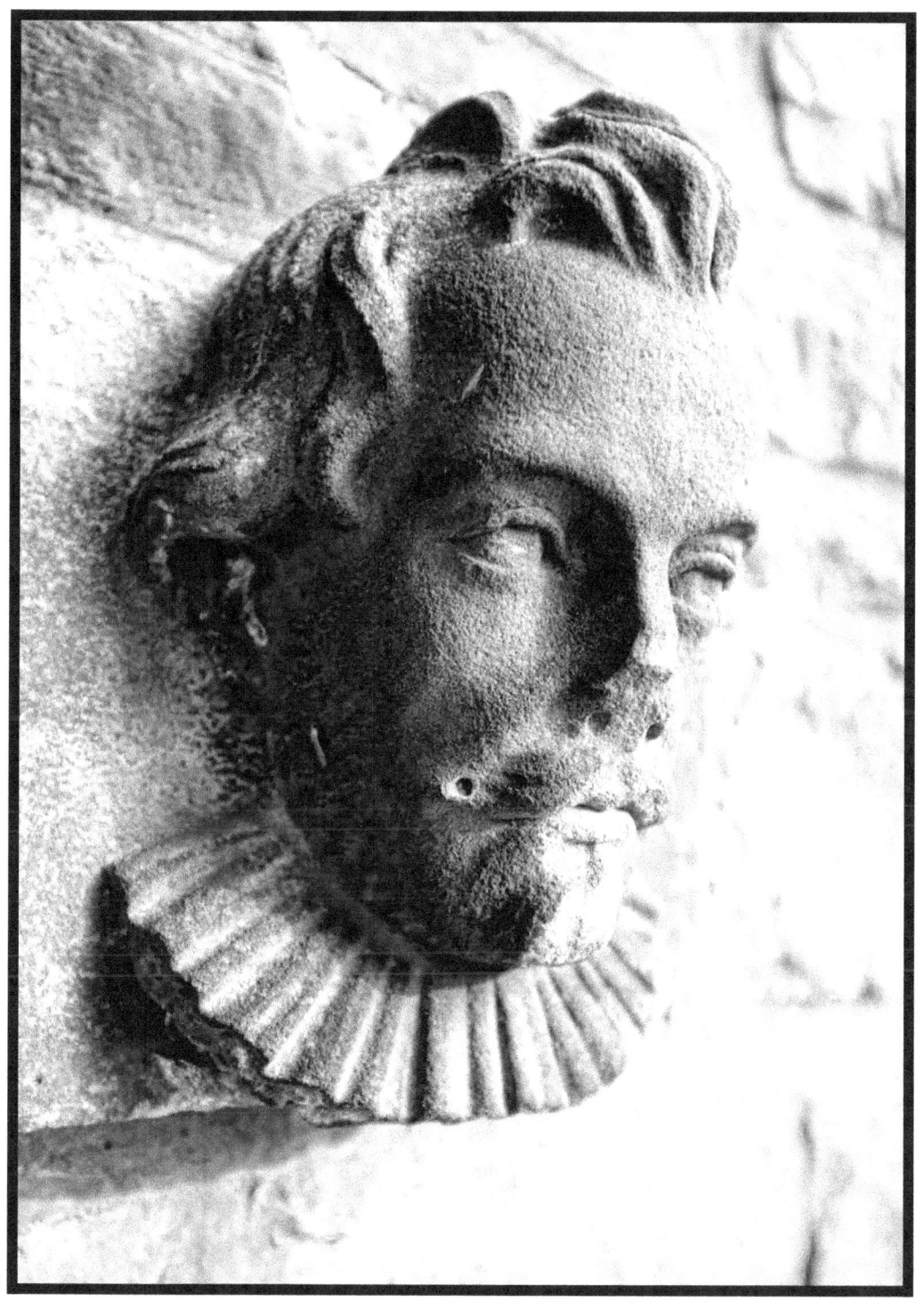

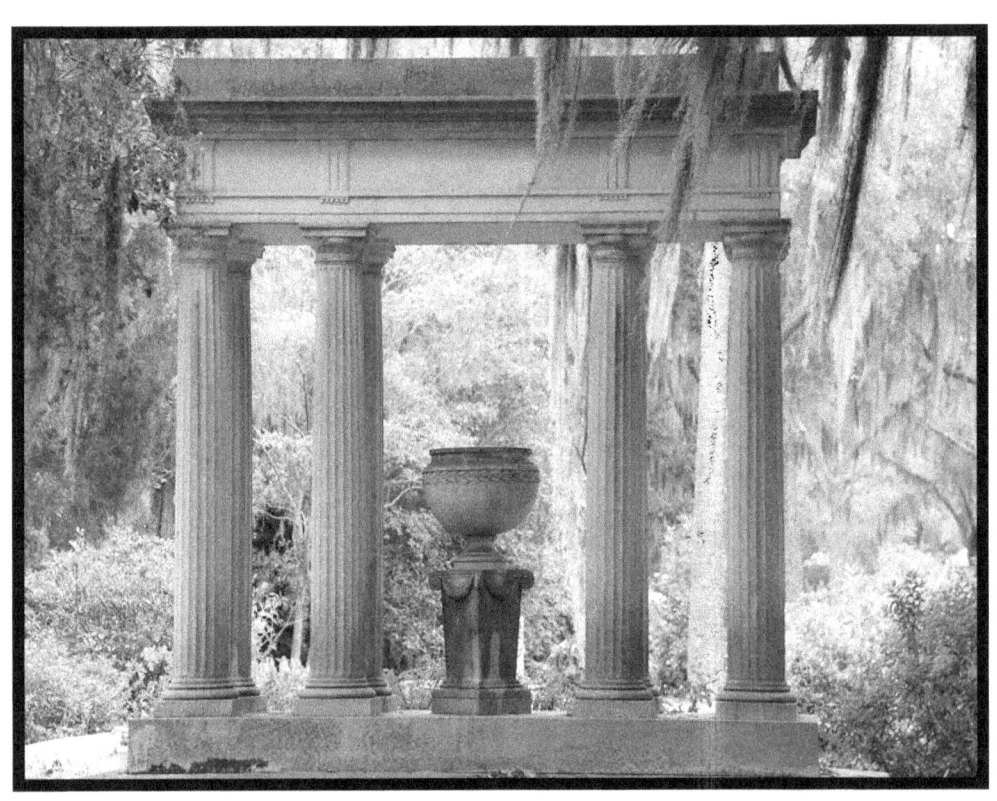

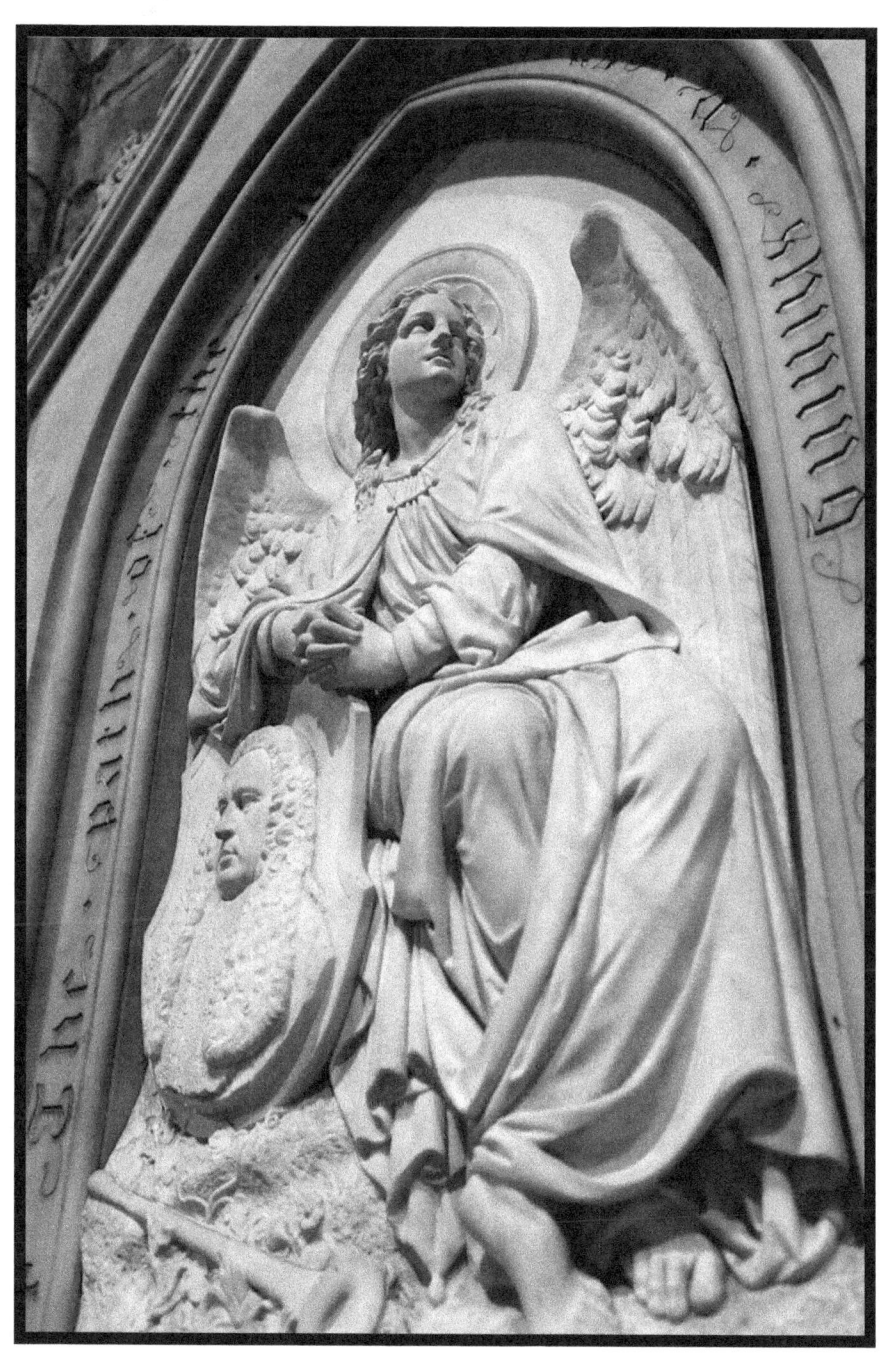

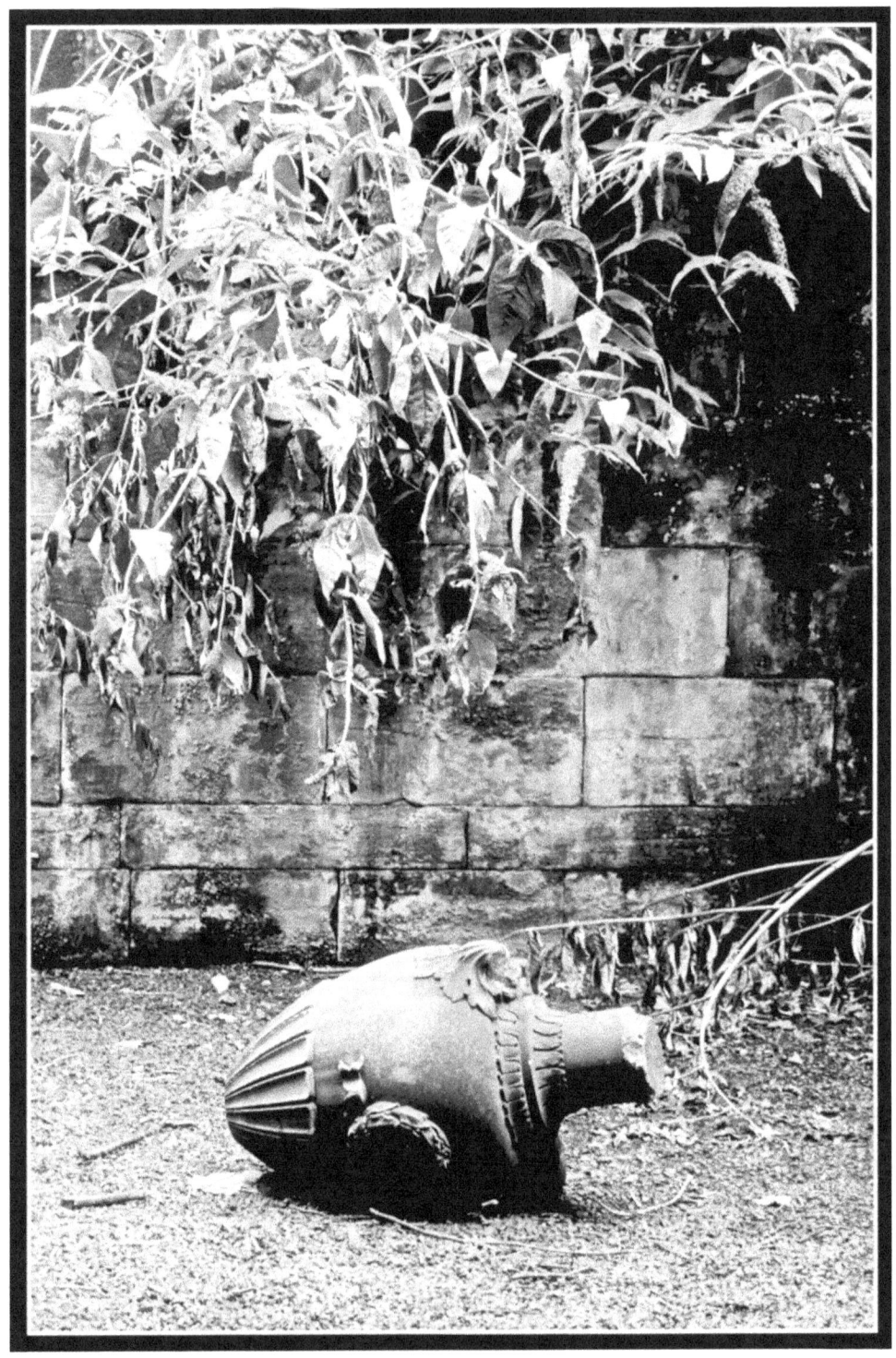

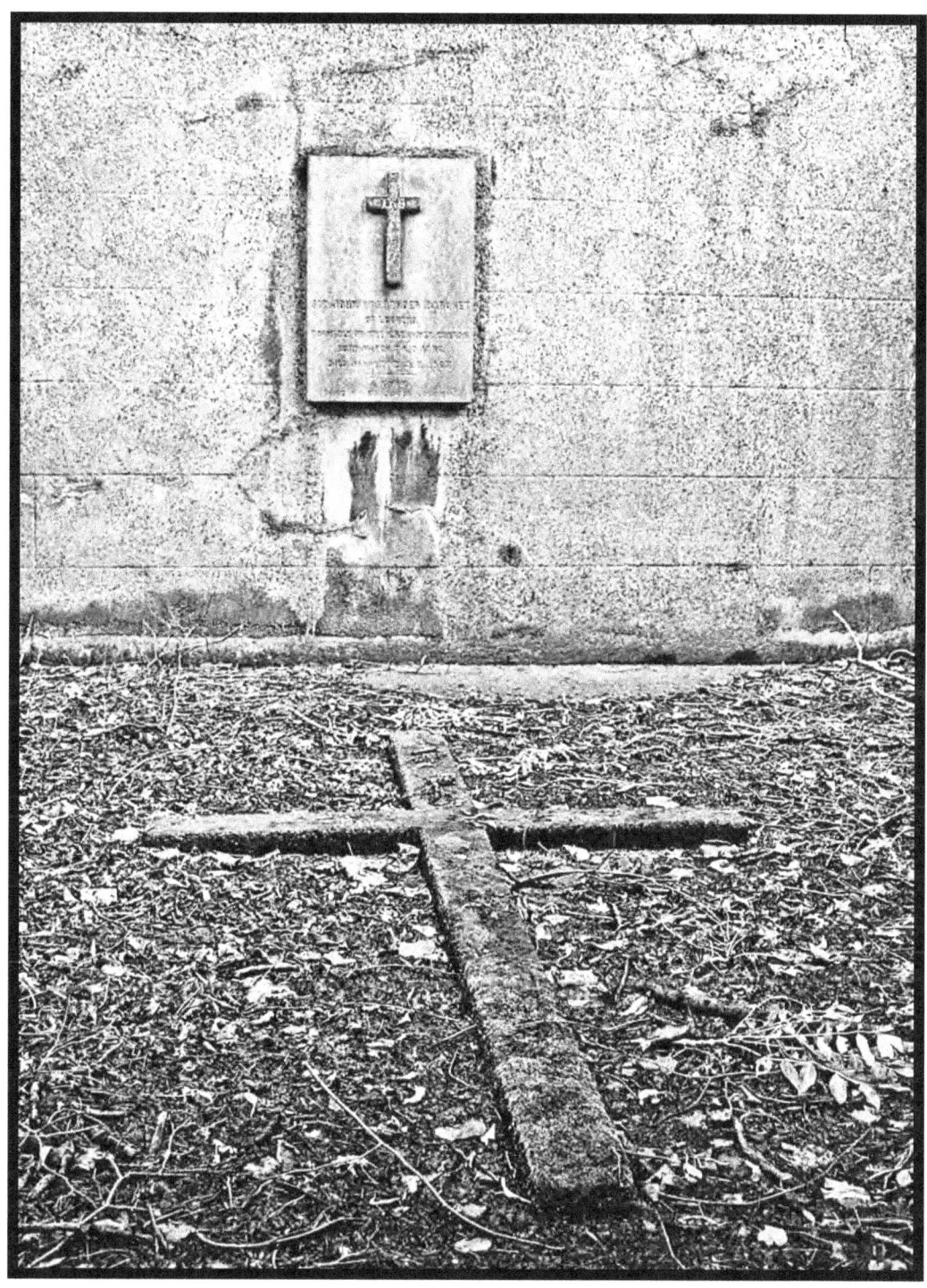

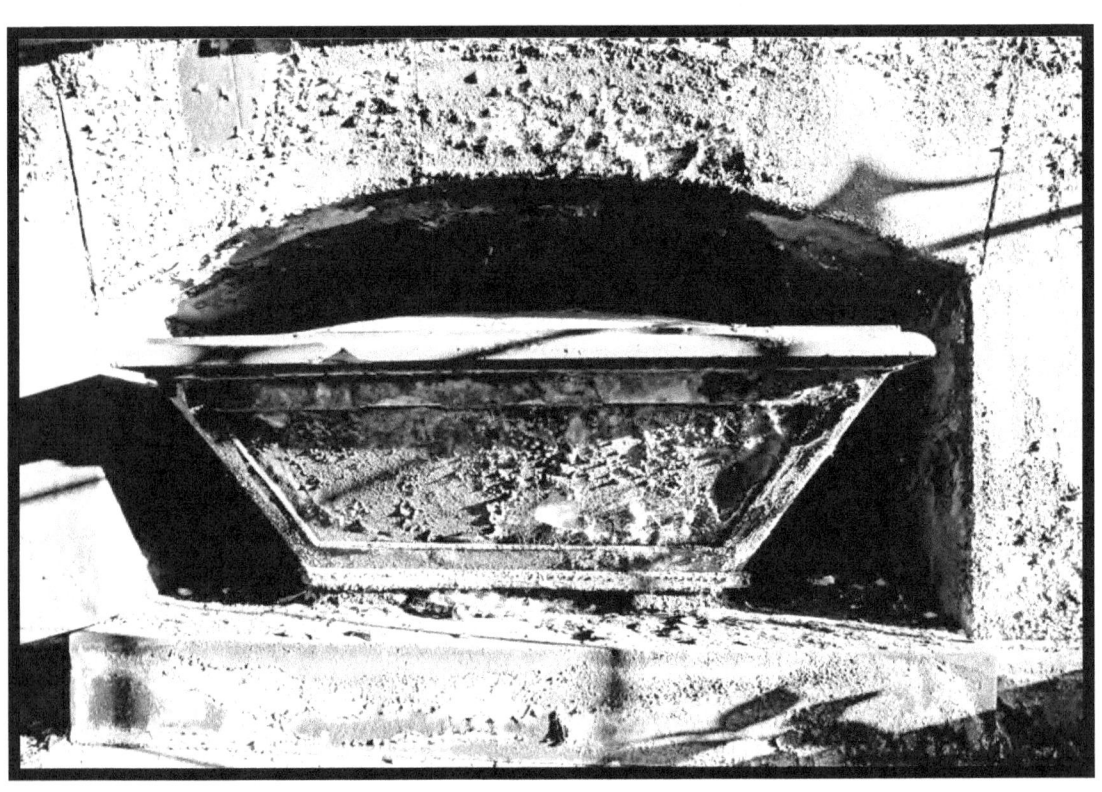

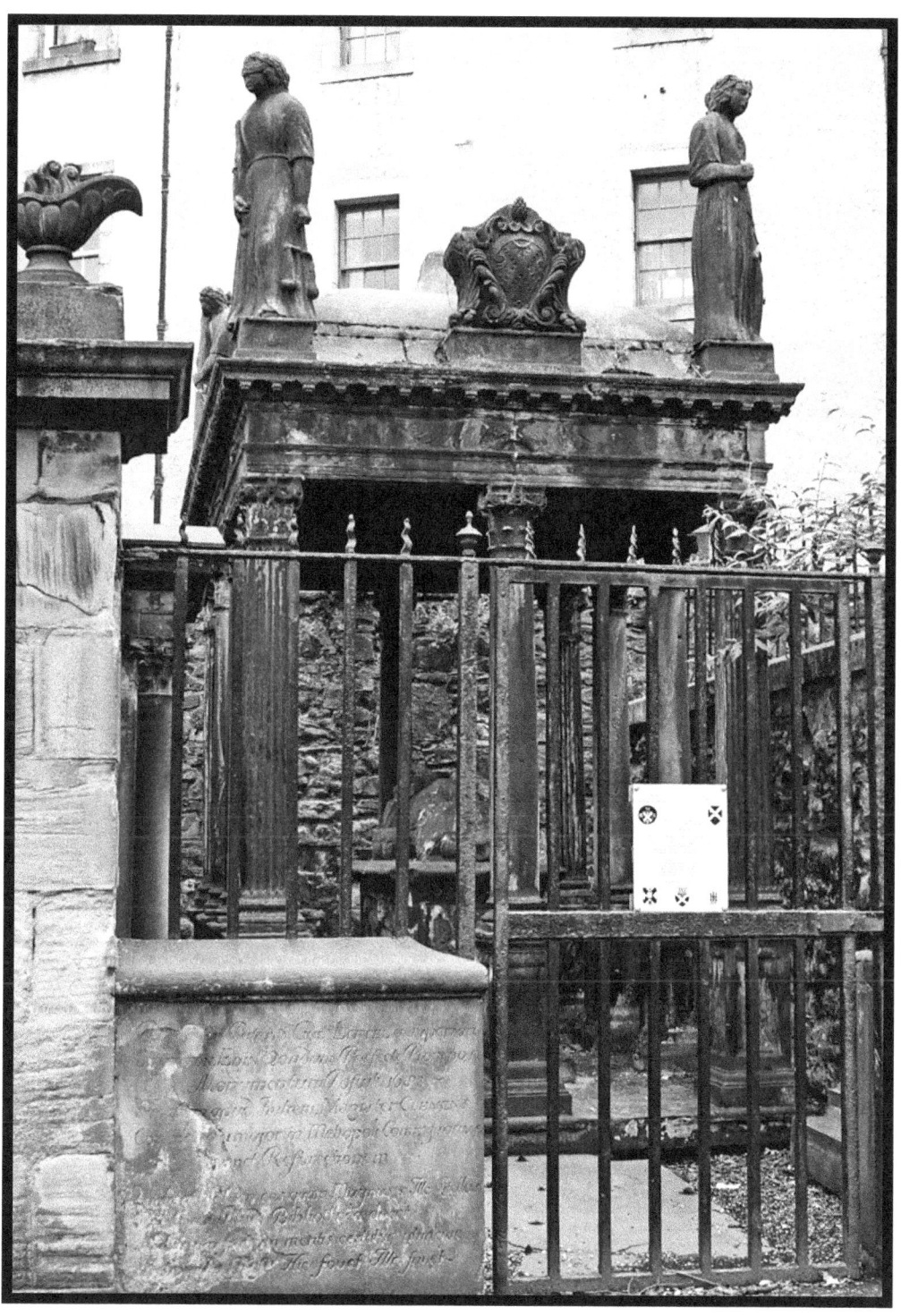

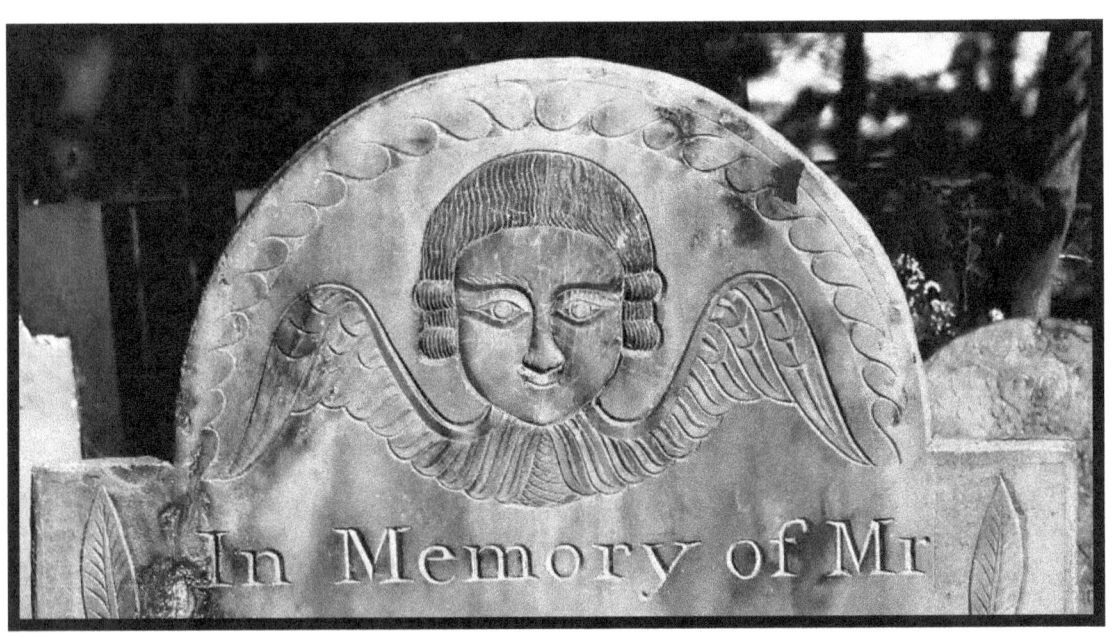

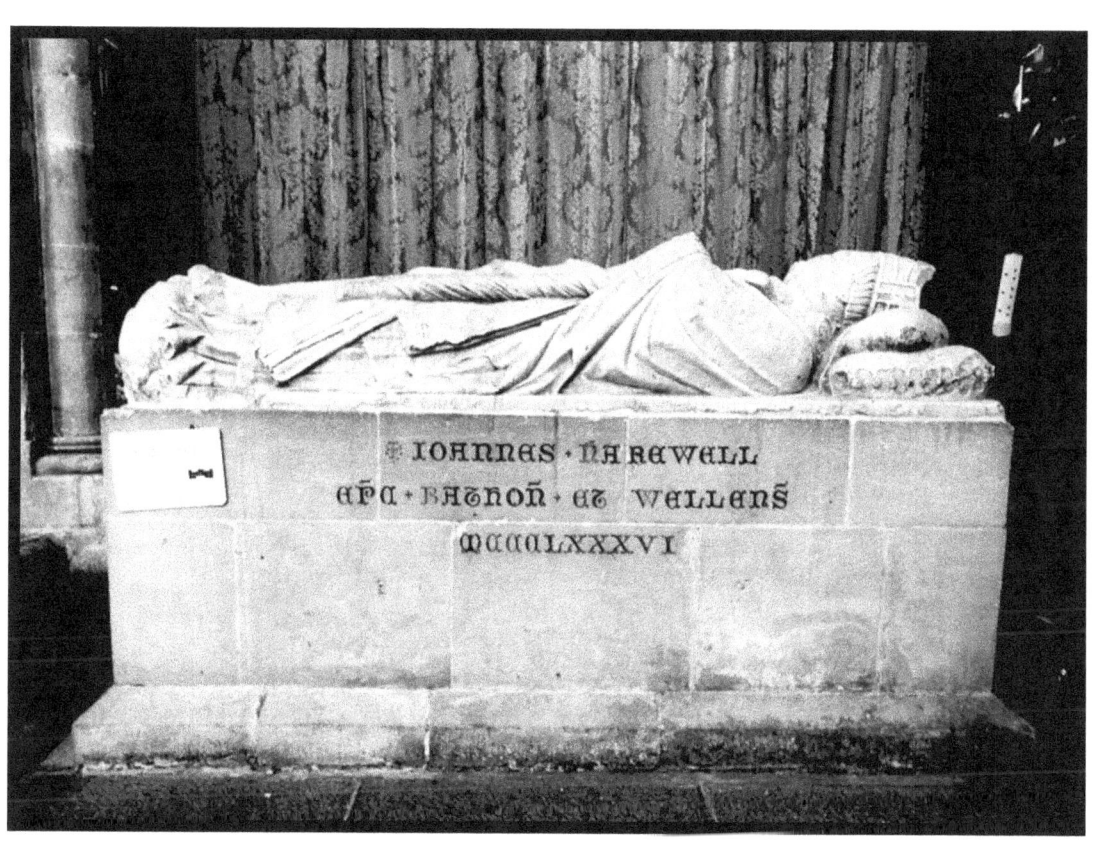

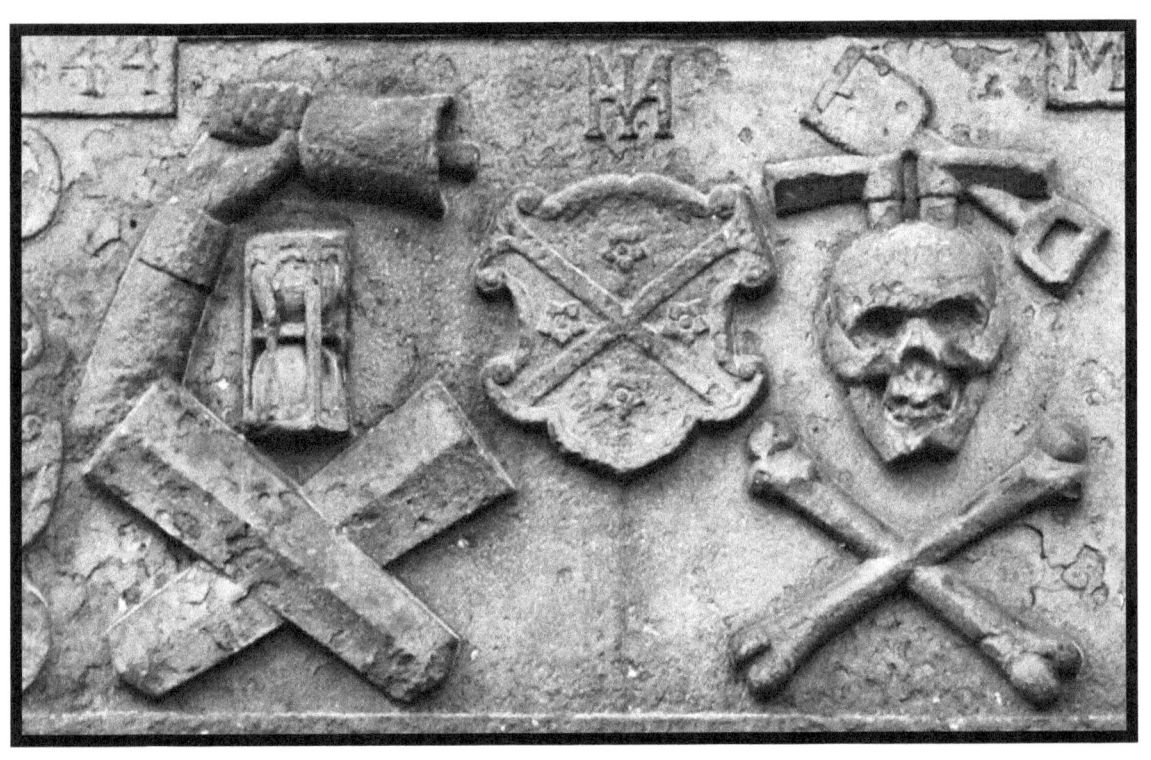

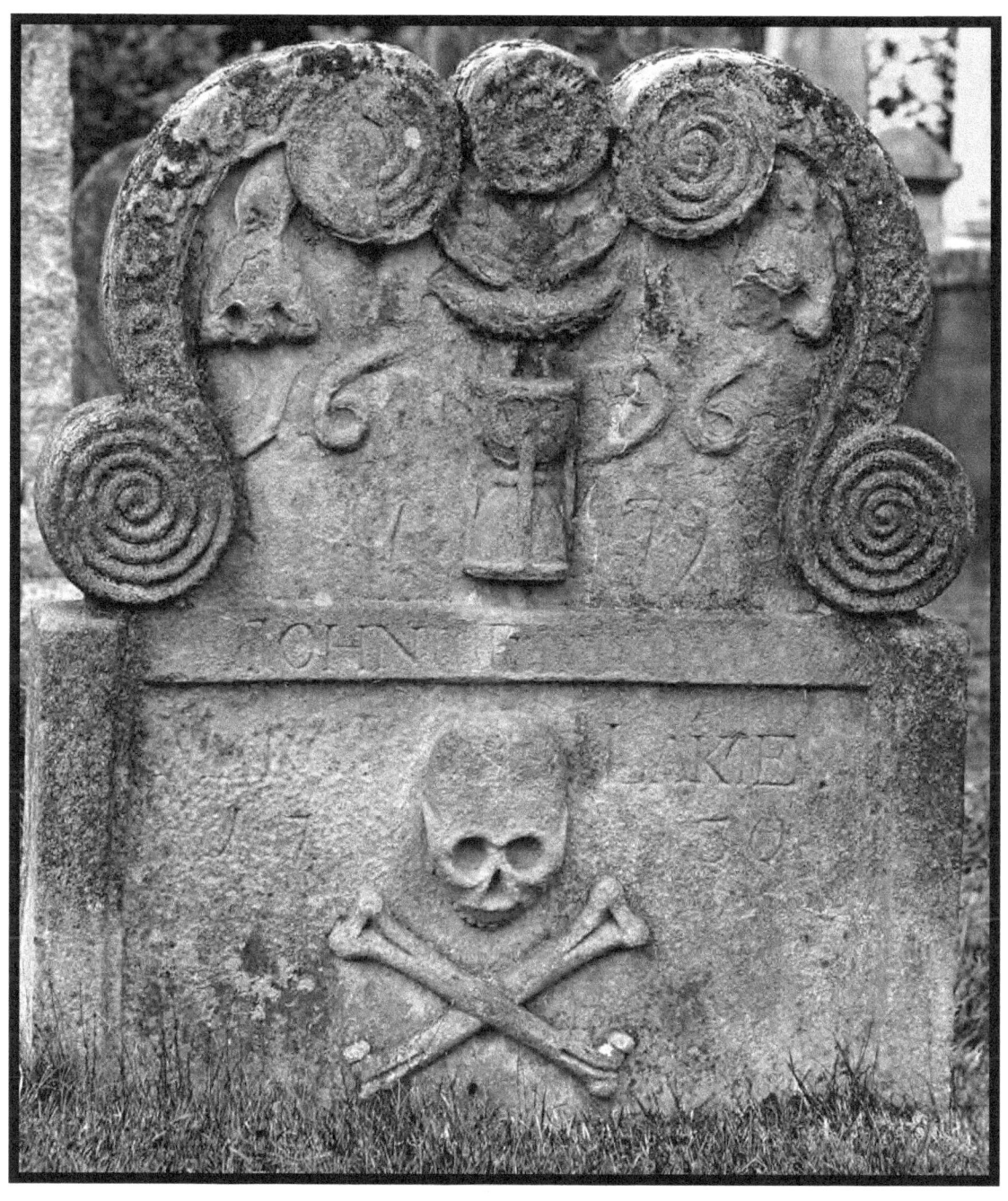

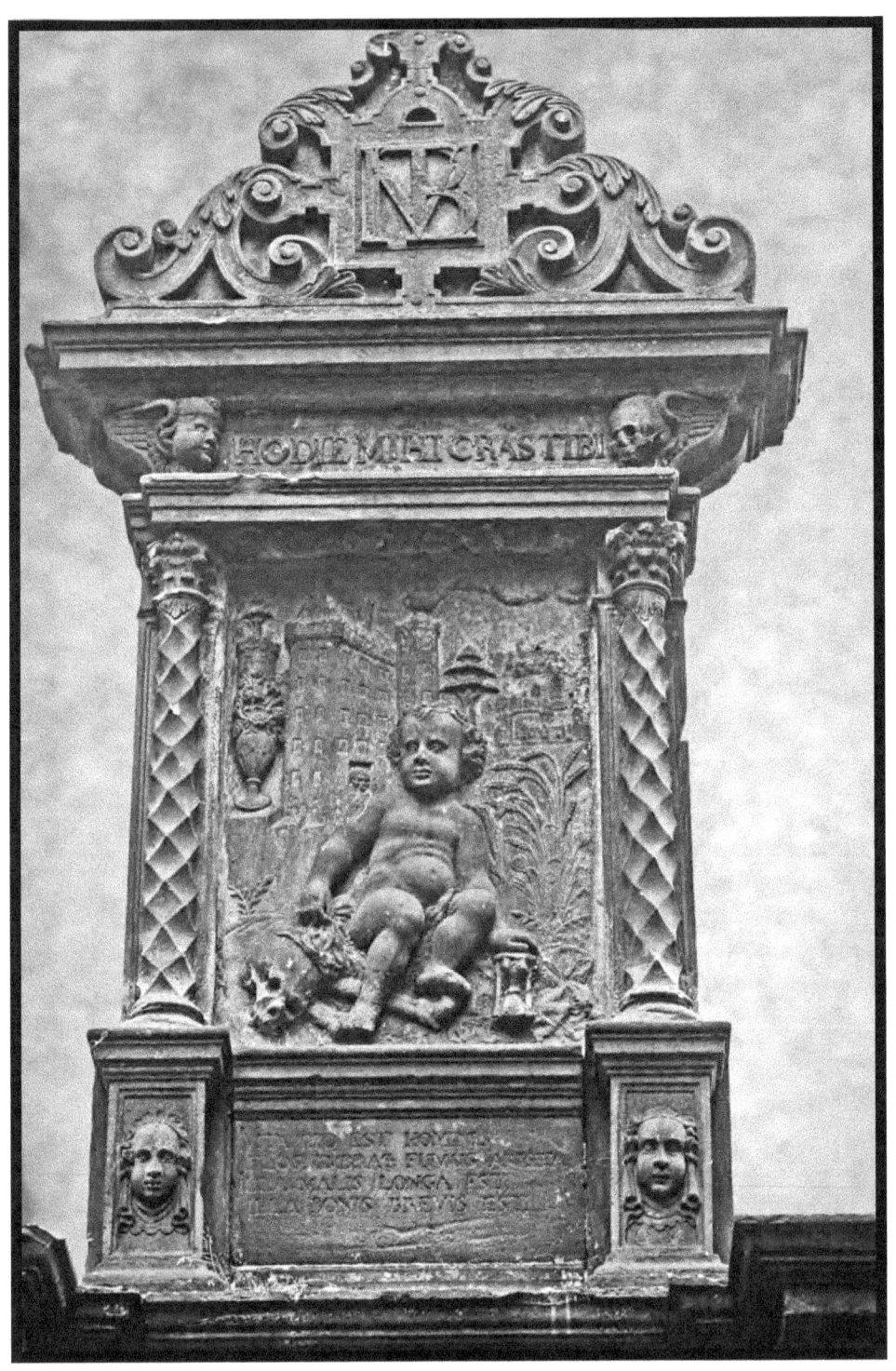

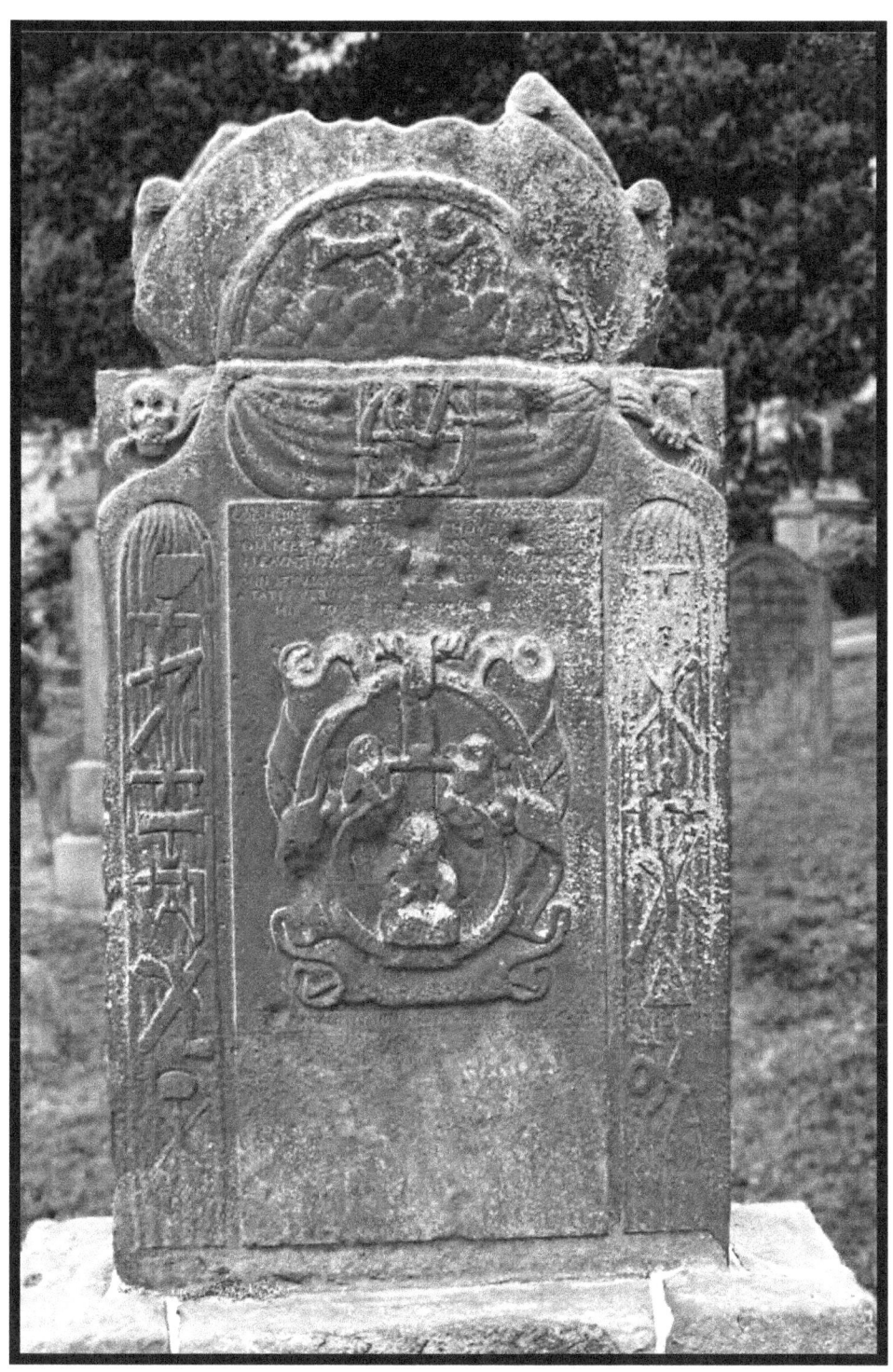

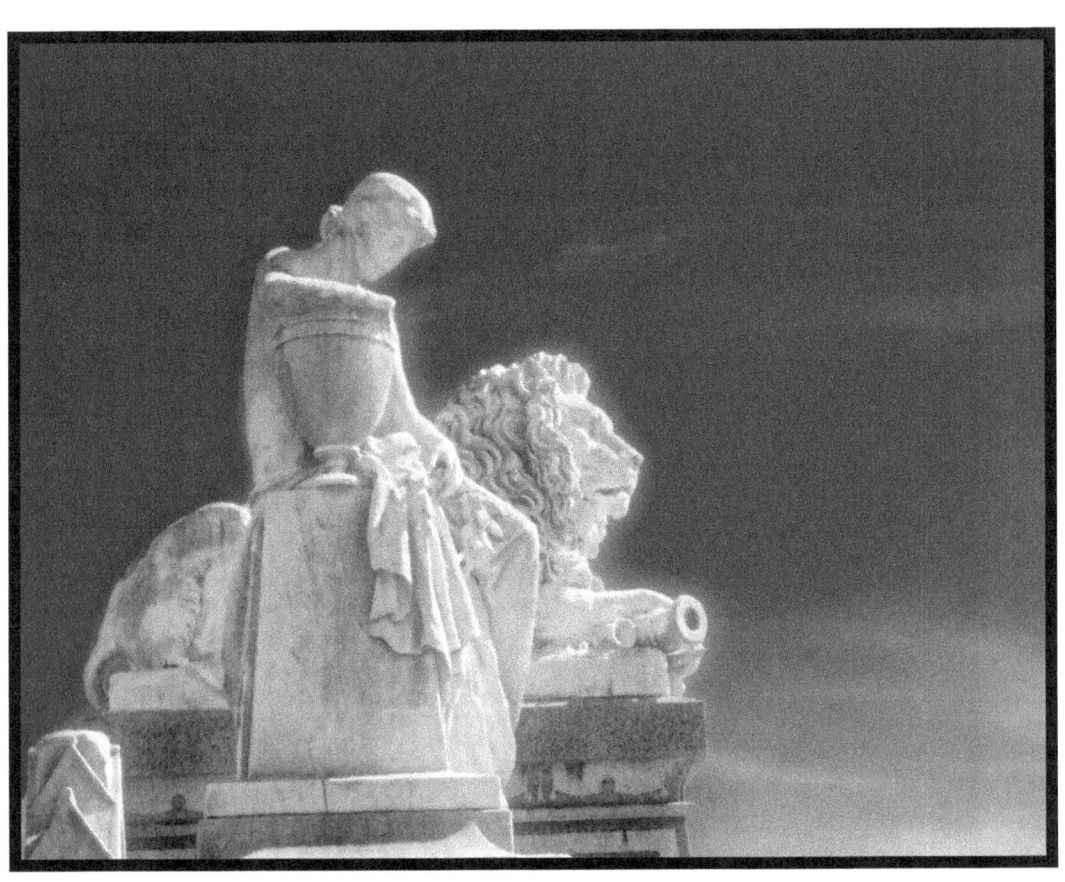

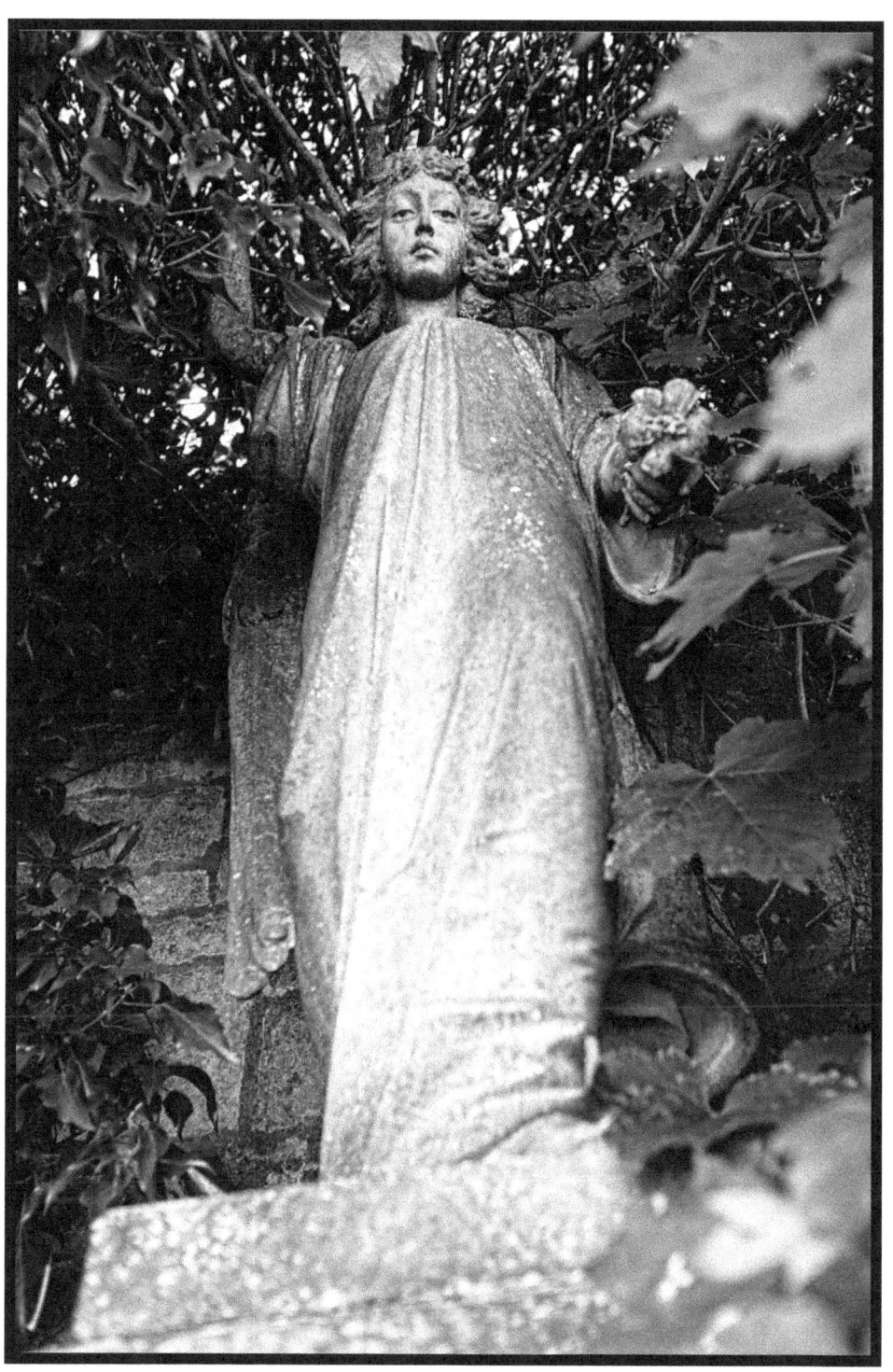

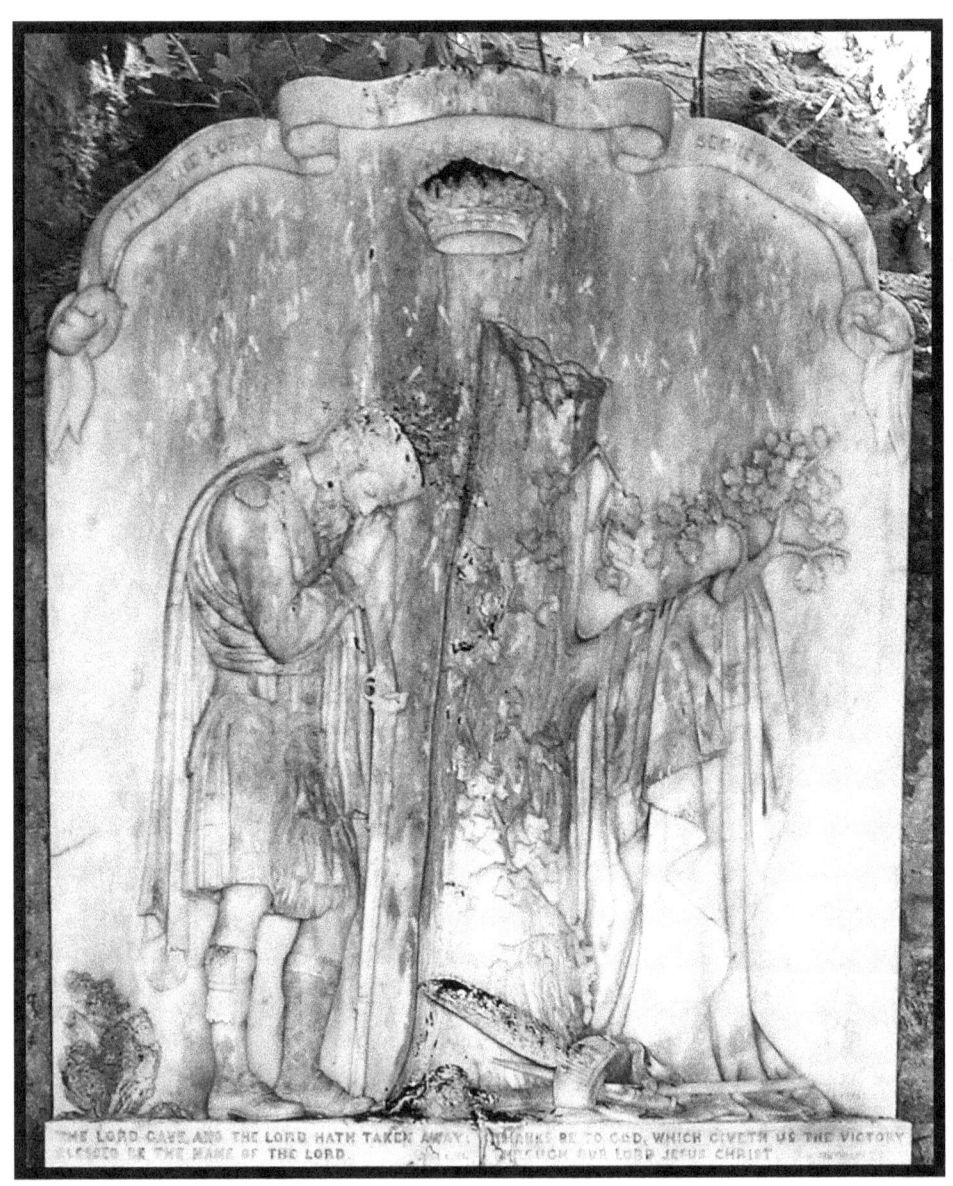

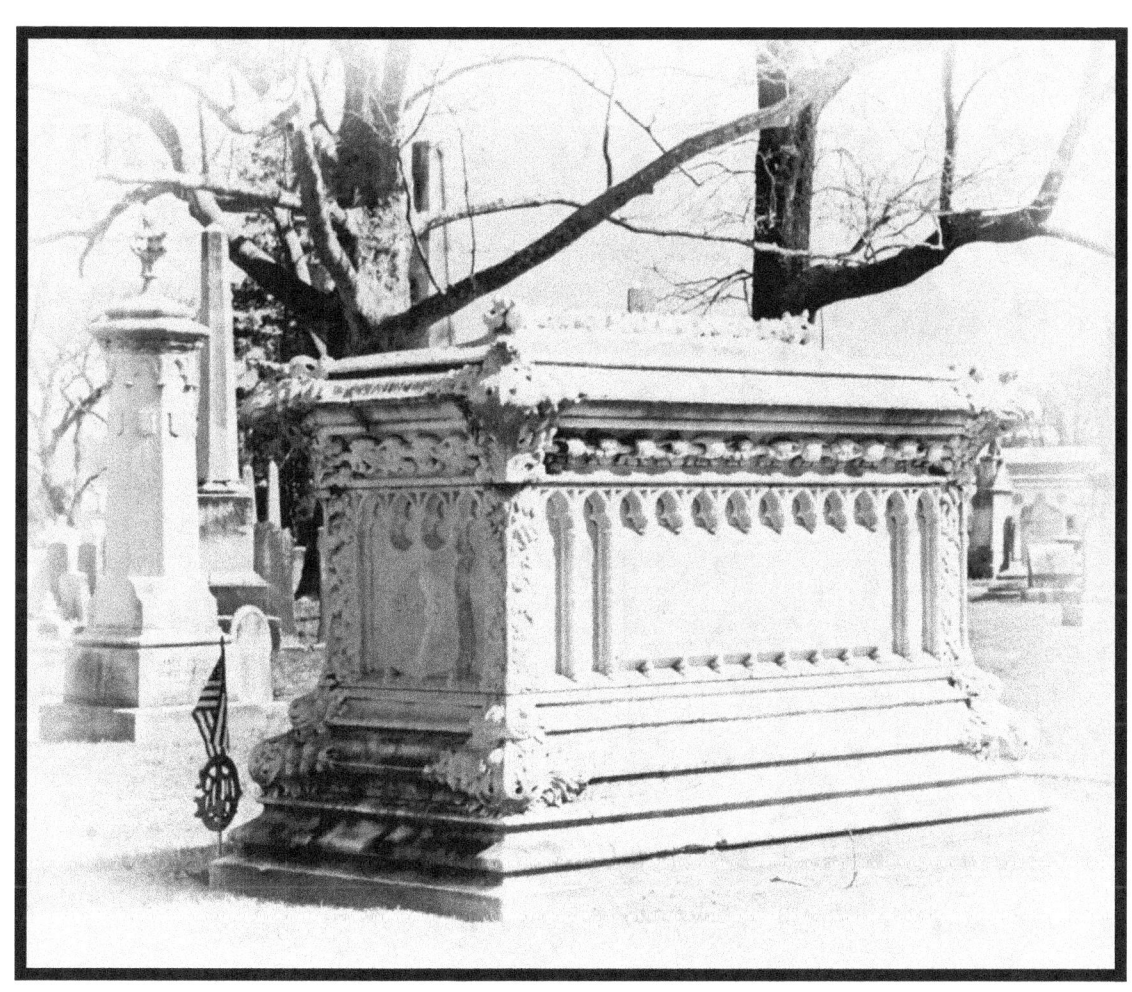

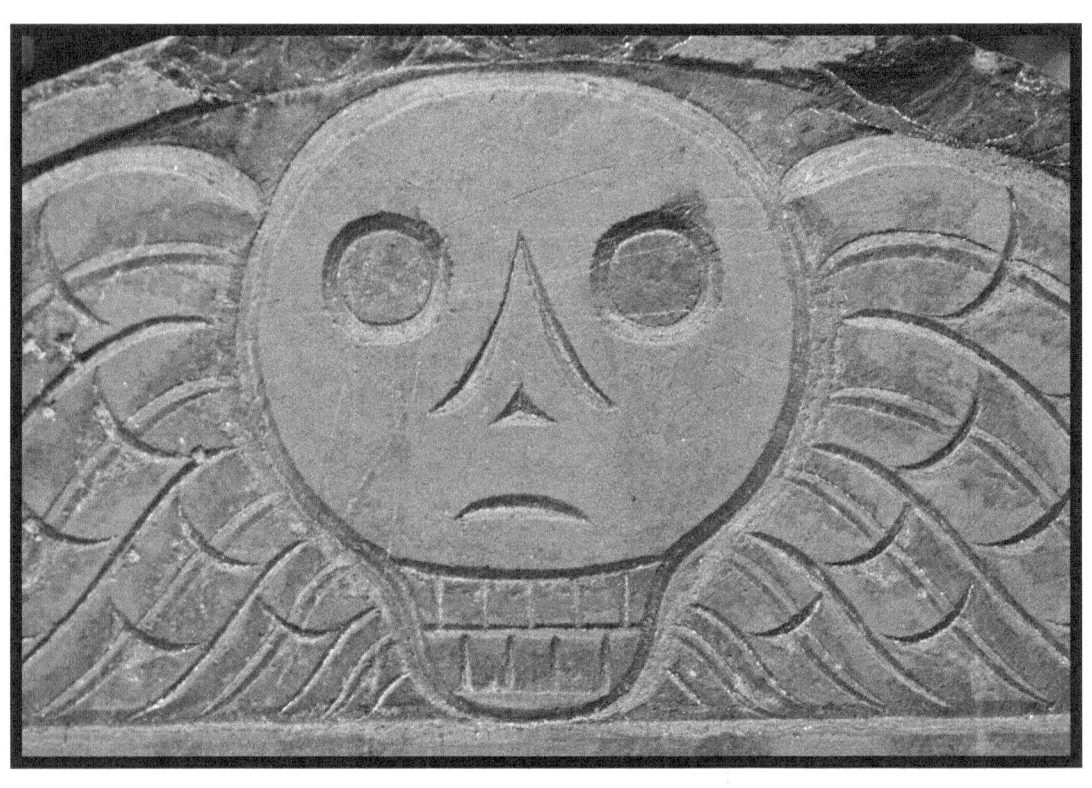

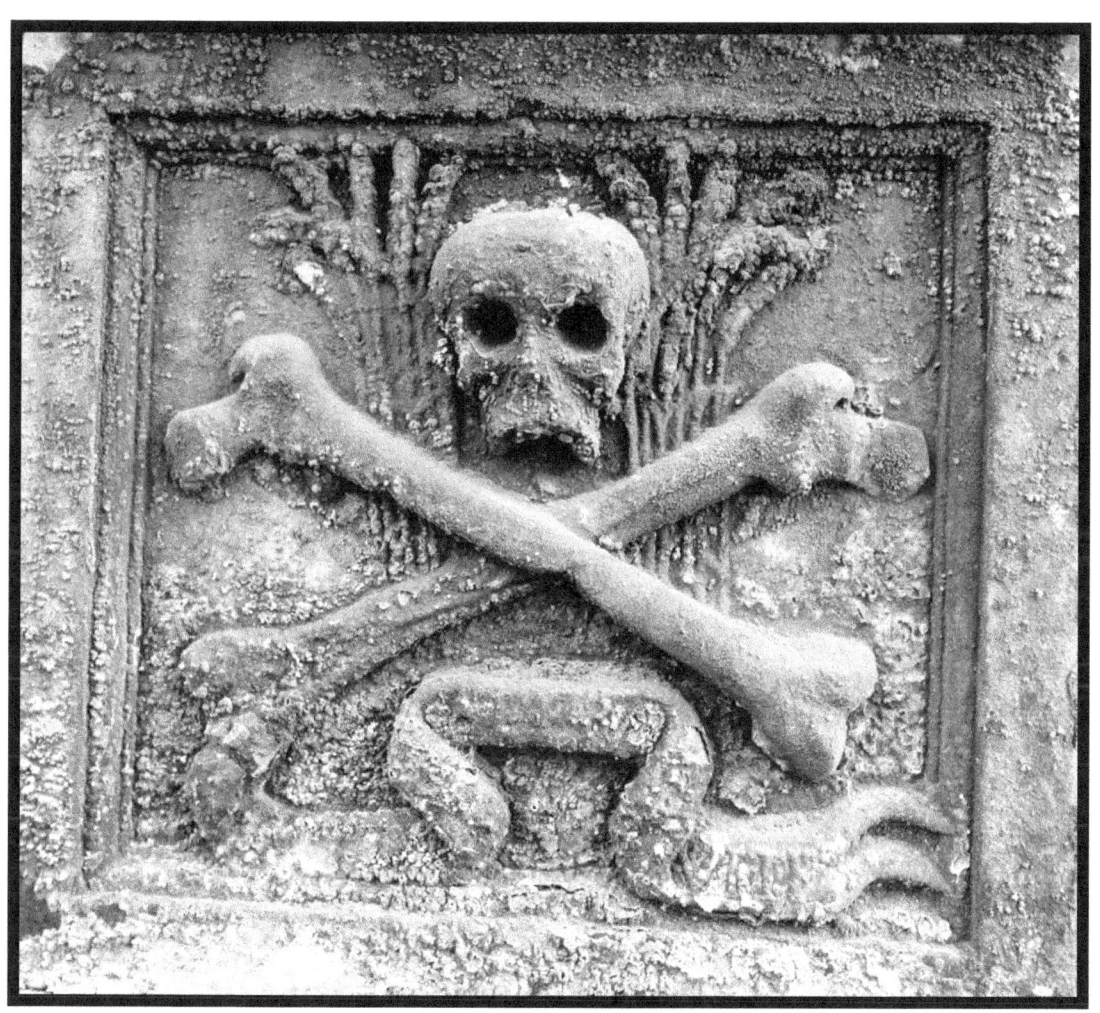

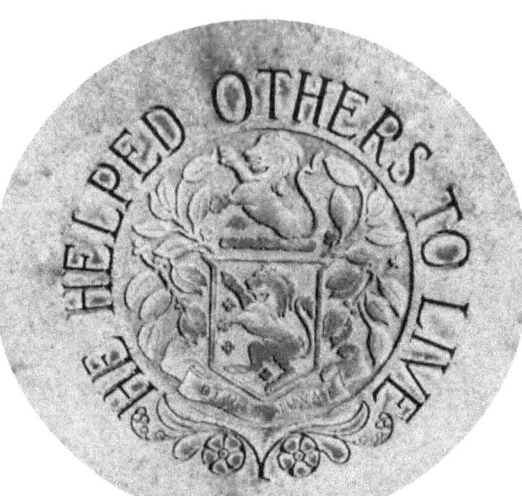

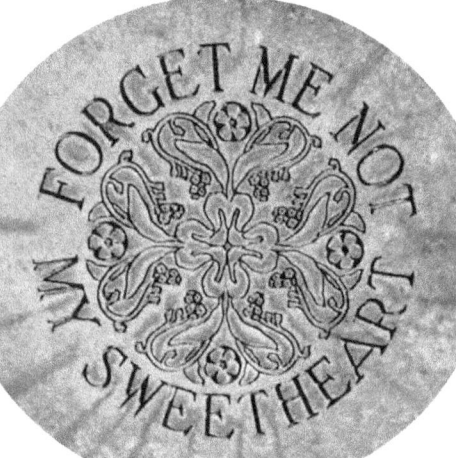

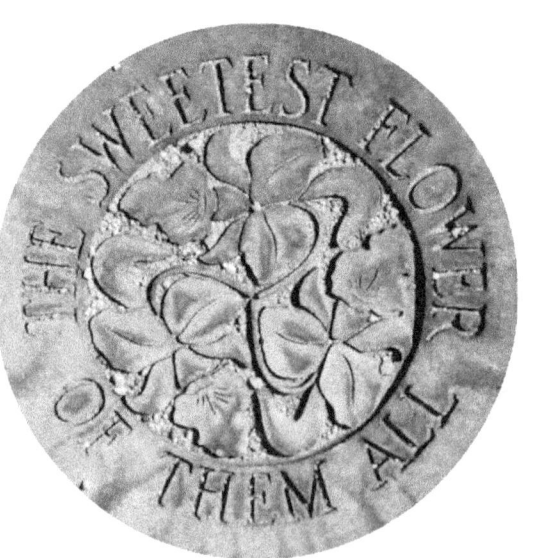

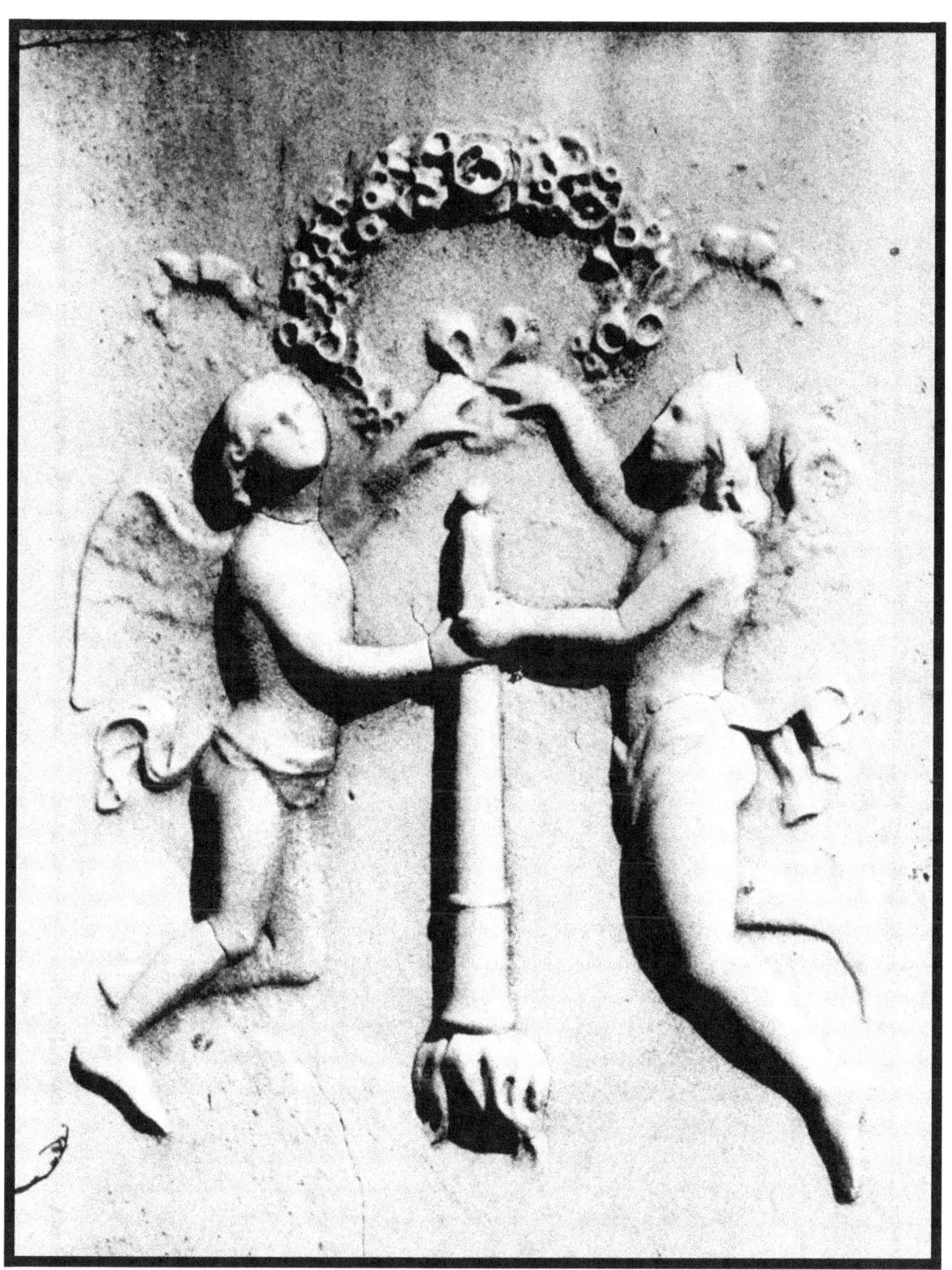

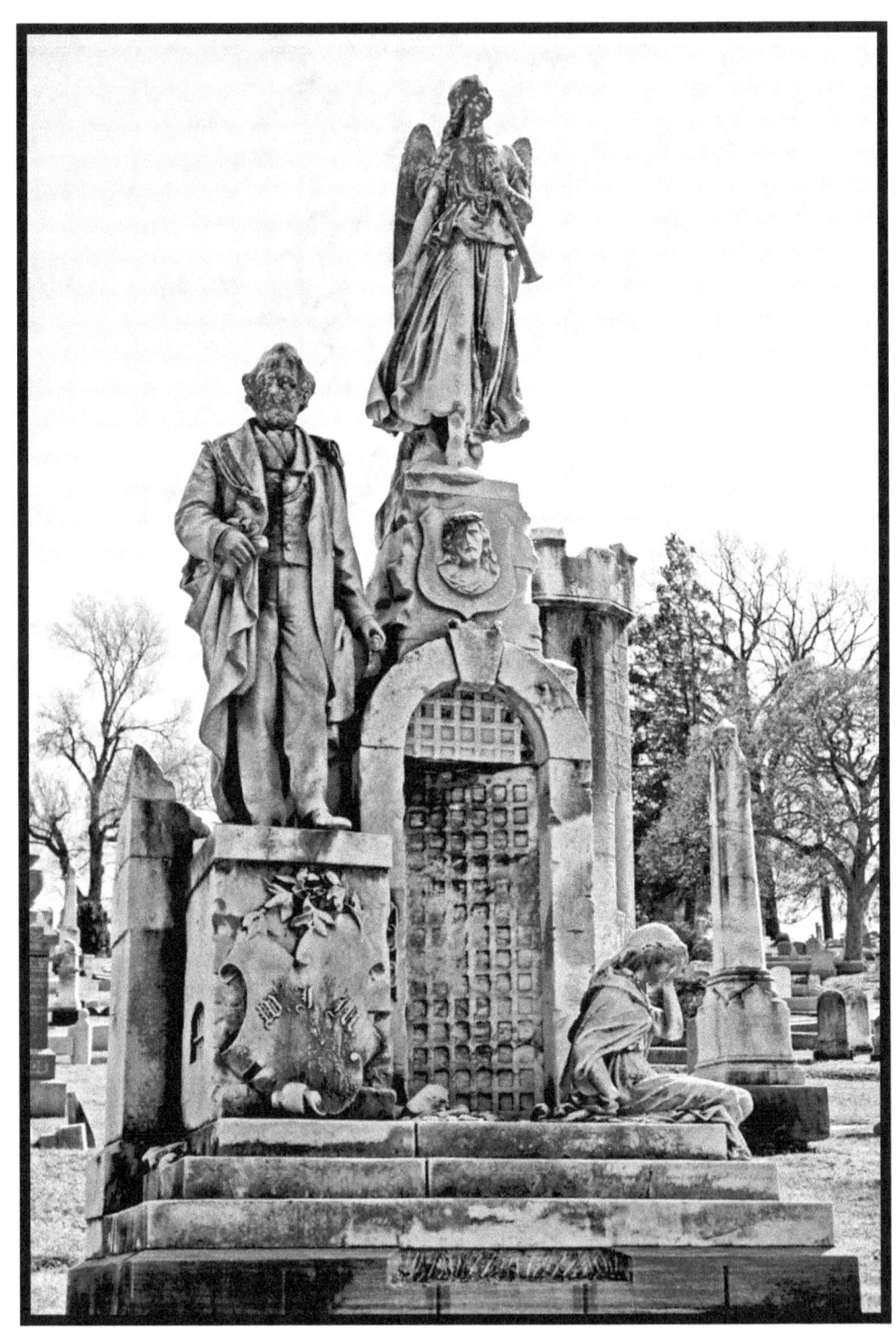

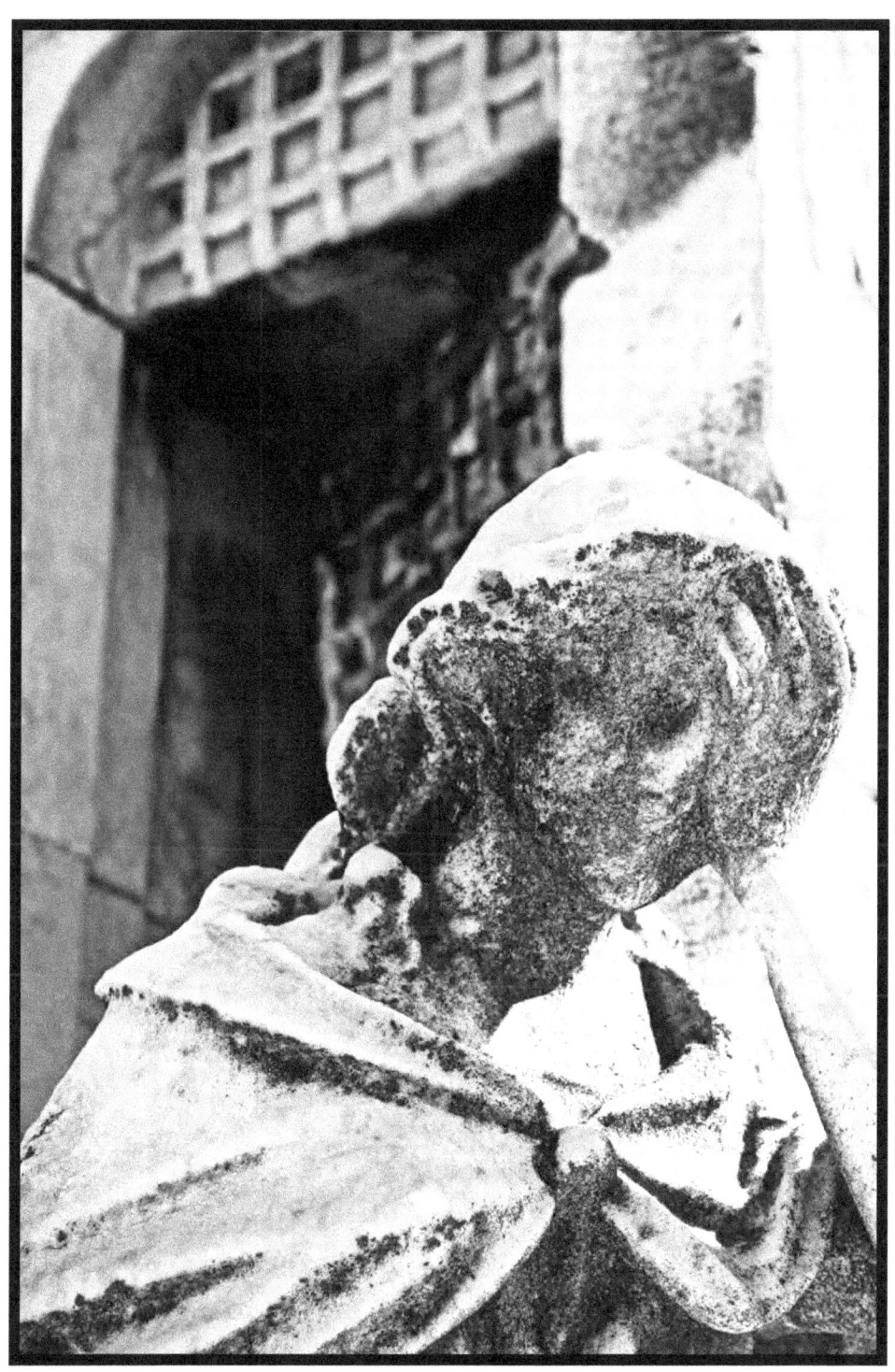

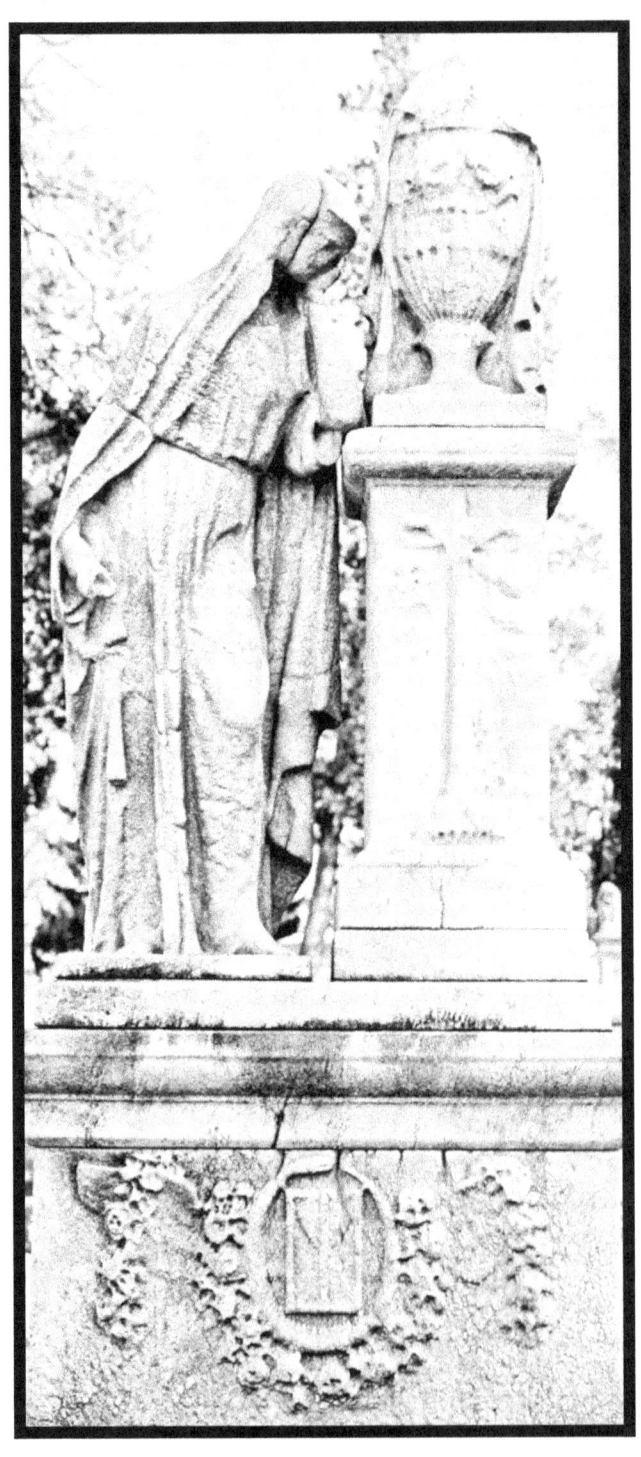

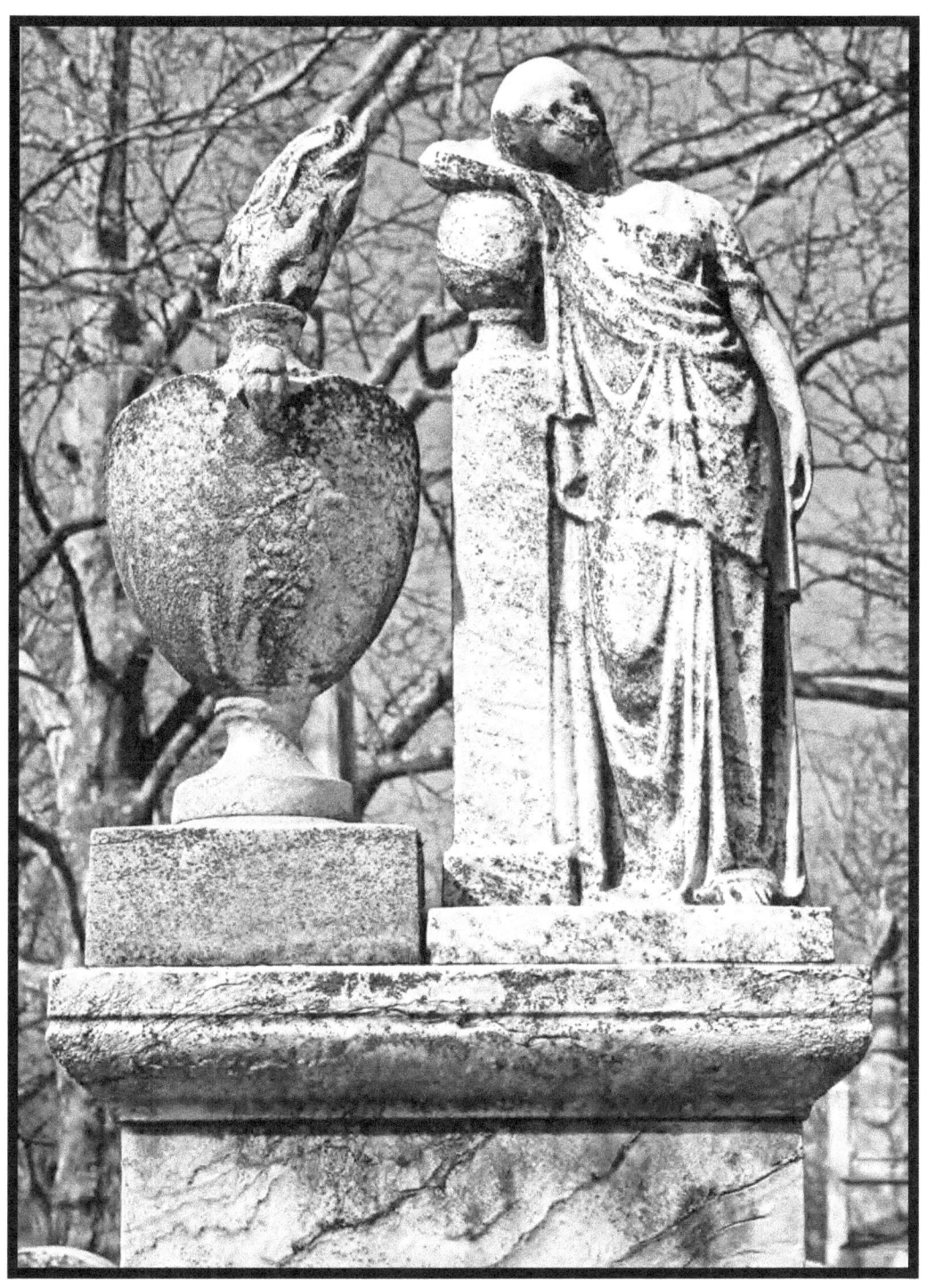

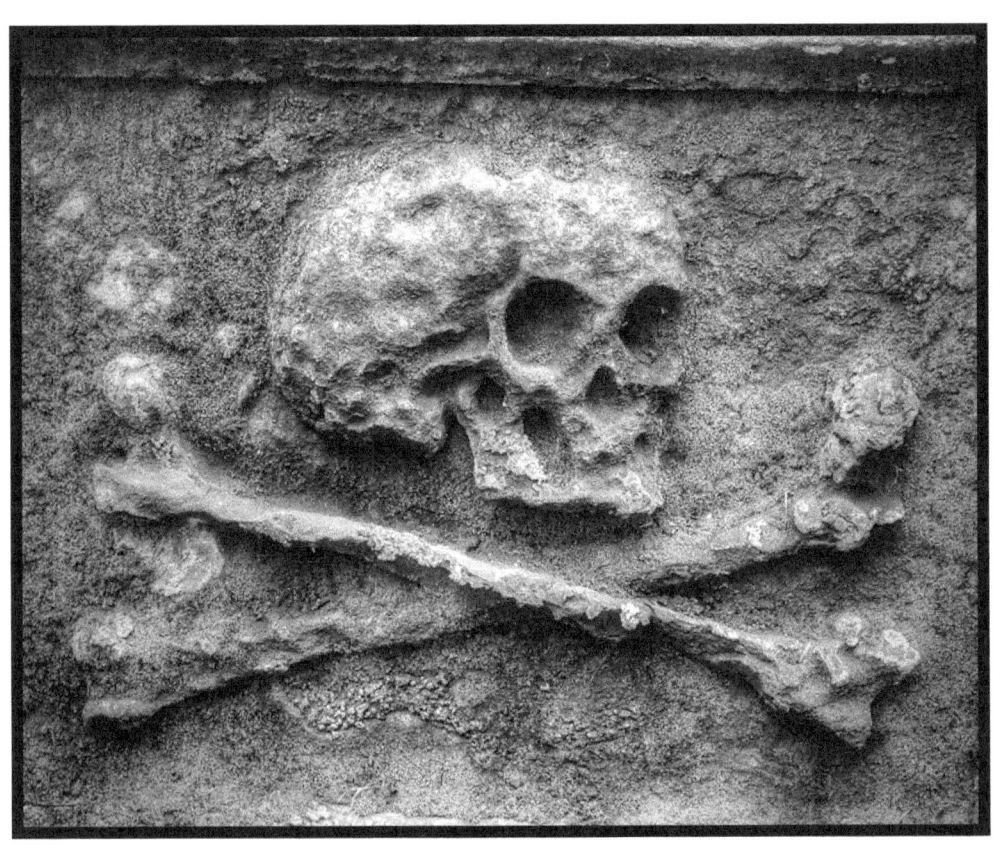

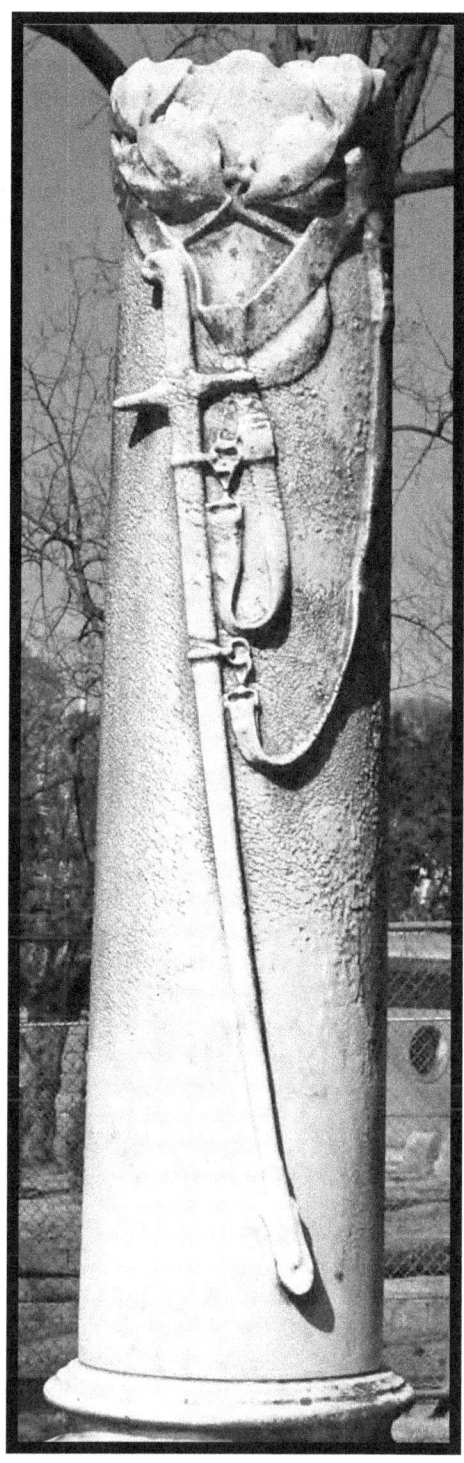

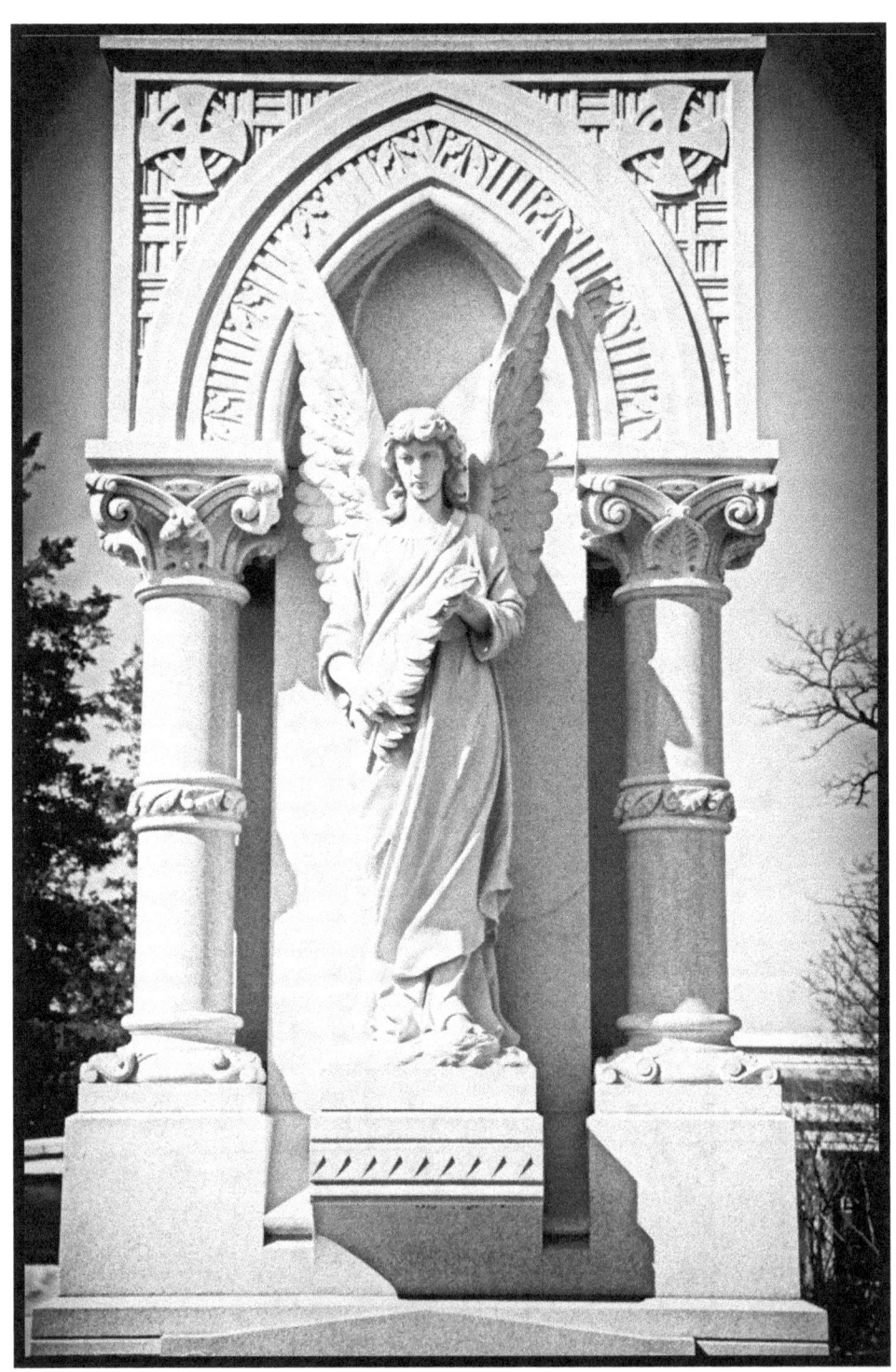

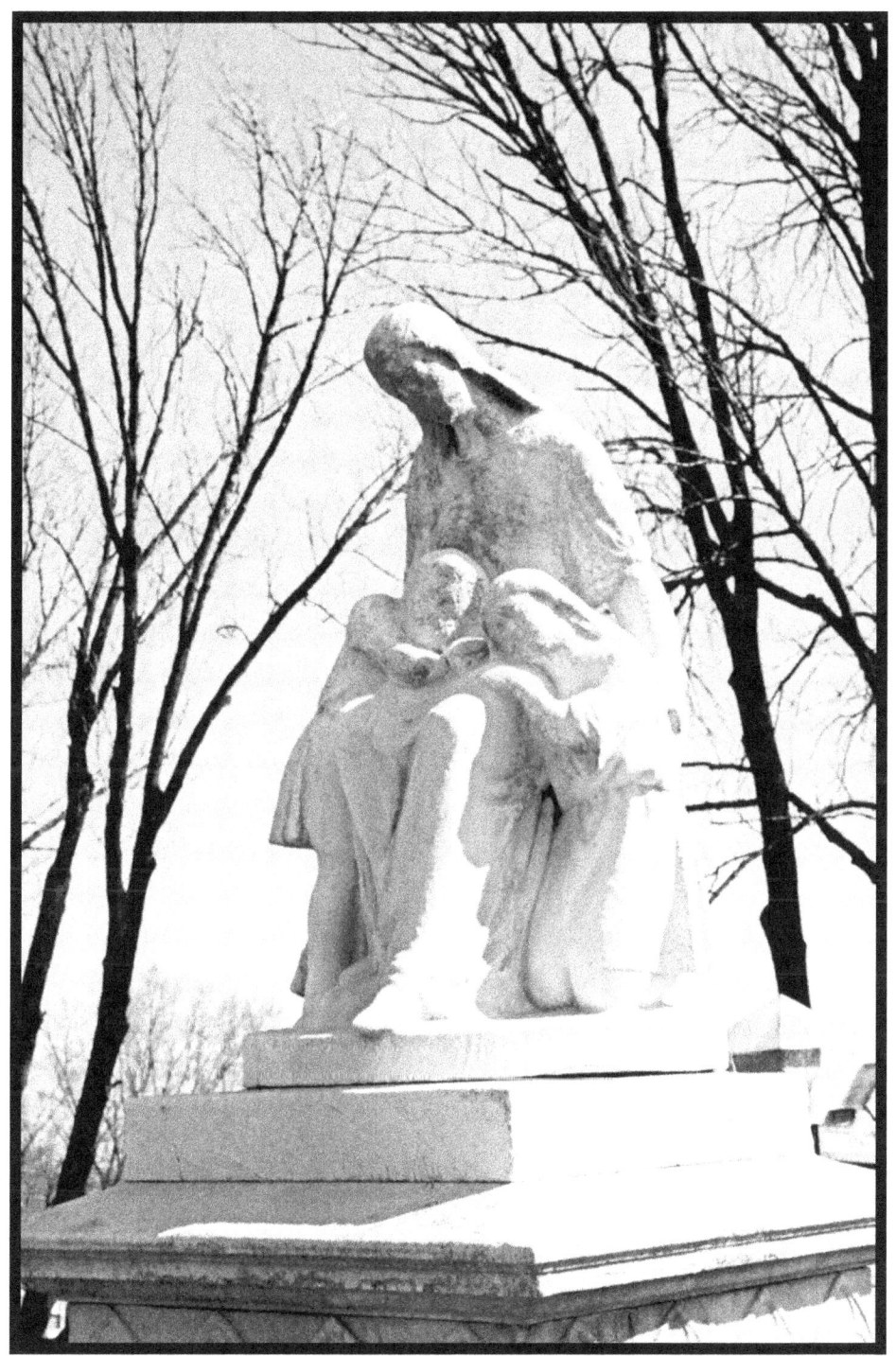

Thank you to all the sites
represented in this book.

Image List

Pg. 34: **Top**: Greyfriars Kirkyard; **Bottom**: Old Town Cemetery, Stirling, Scotland

Pg. 35: Hexham Abbey, Hexham, England

Pg. 36: Rock of Cashel, Tipperary, Ireland

Pg. 37: Jedburgh Abbey, Jedburgh, Scotland

Pg. 38: **Both**: Greyfriars Kirkyard, Edinburgh, Scotland

Pg. 39: Greyfriars Kirkyard, Edinburgh, Scotland

Pg. 40: Bonaventure Cemetery, (near) Savannah, Georgia

Pg. 41: Saint Patrick's Cathedral, Dublin, Ireland

Pg. 42, 43, 44 & 45: Greyfriars Kirkyard, Edinburgh, Scotland

Pg. 46: Burying Point Cemetery, Salem, Massachusetts

Pg. 47: Wells Cathedral, Wells, England

Pg. 48: Greyfriars Kirkyard, Edinburgh, Scotland

Pg. 49: Old Town Cemetery, Stirling, Scotland

Pg. 50: Greyfriars Kirkyard, Edinburgh, Scotland

Pg. 51: Old Town Cemetery, Stirling, Scotland

Pg. 52: Laurel Hill Cemetery, Philadelphia, Pennsylvania

Pg. 53: Roslin Cemetery, Roslin, Scotland (near Rosslyn Chapel)

Pg. 54: St. Brides Kirk, Blair Atholl, Scotland

Pg. 55: Laurel Hill Cemetery, Philadelphia, Pennsylvania

Pg. 56: Burying Point Cemetery, Salem, Massachusetts

Pg. 57: Greyfriars Kirkyard, Edinburgh, Scotland

Pg. 58, 59, 60, 61, 62 & 63: Laurel Hill Cemetery, Philadelphia, Pennsylvania

Pg. 64: Greyfriars Kirkyard, Edinburgh, Scotland

Pg. 65 & 66: Laurel Hill Cemetery, Philadelphia, Pennsylvania

Back Cover: Laurel Hill Cemetery, Philadelphia, Pennsylvania

About the Author:

Traci Law is an award-winning photographer in the Philadelphia area. She has captured images from around the world from landscapes to wildlife and architecture. Whether it be Romania, Australia, Vancouver or Edinburgh, there are few places she has not been and few adventures she has not tried from swimming with sharks in Belize to climbing around ruins in Europe or hunting down the truth behind 'Dracula' in Romania.

When she doesn't have a camera in hand she can often be found on set as an actor, digging in the dirt on an archaeological excavation or chasing down ghosts on a paranormal investigation.

For more information about Traci Law, her art or her other interests visit
www.tracilaw.net

www.ingramcontent.com/pod-product-compliance
Lightning Source LLC
Chambersburg PA
CBHW081602170526
45166CB00009B/2794